# VALUING PEOPLE

# PEOPLE

## HOW HUMAN CAPITAL CAN BE
## YOUR STRONGEST ASSET

## LISA M. ALDISERT

# Dearborn™
### Trade Publishing
A **Kaplan Professional** Company

Acquisitions Editor: Mary B. Good
Senior Managing Editor: Jack Kiburz
Cover Design: Design Solutions
Interior Design: Lucy Jenkins
Typesetting: the dotted i

© 2002 by Lisa M. Aldisert

Published by Dearborn Trade Publishing, a Kaplan Professional Company

Printed in the United States of America

02   03   04      10  9   8   7   6   5   4   3   2   1

**Library of Congress Cataloging-in-Publication Data**
Aldisert, Lisa M., 1954-
    Valuing people : how human capital can be your strongest asset /
Lisa M. Aldisert.
        p.      cm.
    Includes index.
    ISBN 0-7931-5015-9
    1. Human capital.    2. Human capital—Evaluation.    3. Personnel
management.    4. Career development.    5. Corporations—Valuation.
I. Title.
HD4904.7 .A437   2002
658.3—dc21                                              2002001823


Dearborn Trade books are available at special quantity discounts to use for sales promotions, employee premiums, or educational purposes. Please call our Special Sales Department to order or for more information, at 800-621-9621, ext. 4307, or write Dearborn Trade Publishing, 155 N. Wacker Drive, Chicago, IL 60606-1719.

# ACKNOWLEDGMENTS

My first awareness about the importance of valuing and measuring human capital occurred when I was a banker. I was rebuffed by a traditional asset-based credit officer for placing so much reliance on people's ability to generate cash flow for loan repayments. His opinion may have had merit in the industrial era but was outdated in the service economy and the newly emerging knowledge economy. I extend my thanks to banking colleagues for igniting my curiosity about how to value human capital and other intangible assets.

Many people were generous in sharing their ideas as *Valuing People: How Human Capital Can Be Your Strongest Asset* came to fruition. A number of experts who are pioneers in valuing intangibles—including human assets—contributed their expertise and opinions. I extend thanks to Catherine Banat, Laurie Bassi, Bill Bonnstetter, Bill Brooks, Chris Browne, Baruch Lev, Bob Elliott, John Hover, Dan Pink, and Rob Williams for the value they added to the project. I also thank Gary Antonick, Linda Bergen, Jan Hoffmeister, Terri Lonier, Barbara Maddock, Dave Near, Jeff Schmidt, and Pat Ward for their leadership in this arena.

I offer thanks to Leigh Talmage, Vikki Brock, and my parents, Agatha and Rugi Aldisert, who are always willing to listen to my ideas and encourage my writing. They contributed their wisdom by reading the manuscript and making valuable suggestions. My thanks to Bette Price for introducing me to Dearborn Trade Publishing, as well as for frequently and cheerfully checking in by e-mail. I extend thanks to Edie Weiner and Arnold Brown for shaping me into a futurist and for their leadership in strategic trends analysis.

Other friends, family, and colleagues were supportive in a lot of little ways that made a big difference. I extend thanks to Greg and Harley Aldisert, Bob Baxter, Sandy Brophy, Robin Cohn, Jamie Cuneen, Donna Gunter, Robin Graham, Nina Kaufman, Gerry Knorr, Barbara Labatt-Simon, Arthur Levin, Ron Paltrowitz, Amelia Panico, Michael Rhoads, Dave Rosenbaum, Linda Siderius, Mike Tokarz, and Joan Zimmerman.

Mary B. Good, acquisitions editor at Dearborn Trade Publishing, was a partner from the beginning. Her guidance and encouragement were invaluable, as she helped fine-tune the concept and shepherded the project from proposal through completion. The entire team at Dearborn was terrific, offering fresh ideas and support. It is a joy to work with top-notch professionals, and I thank all of them for their contributions.

Finally, I extend thanks to my husband, Batt Johnson, who bolstered me as I went through periods of "extreme focus." I thank him for his patience, encouragement, and good humor.

# CONTENTS

Do you know that you can measure how your people directly impact the value of your company? It's true. But you need to think beyond conventional financial reporting. You won't find it in traditional valuation methods. It doesn't show up in book value. It may be implied in market value. It may be a primary reason behind your firm's cash flow growth. No matter which method of valuation you use, the way a firm values its people directly correlates with how the market values that firm.

Attention getting, isn't it? What this means is that corporate adages, such as "People are our greatest asset" and "We value our people above everything else," can be true and not just hollow phrases in a mission statement. These truths are the keys to your company's value and success. It is up to you to take your key and unlock the potential in your people so that they perform at their highest potential. This will be highly rewarding for them. And it will create more wealth for your firm.

It is hoped that thinking of your people as a driver of corporate value is not a new thought. The idea of human capital as a productive asset that can be enhanced and accounted for, on the other hand, may be new. Under conventional balance sheet accounting, people show up indirectly as short-term and long-term liabilities (wages, benefits, and pensions payable). On the income statement, they represent an expense, again in the form of wages and benefits. To understand how your people create value, the first thing you need to do is stop thinking of them as expenses, which is an outdated thought from the industrial and manufacturing era when labor equaled expense.

Today most firms are knowledge based. They are driven by ideas and concepts, not processes and machines. Being knowledge based doesn't mean that they are in the information technology business. Knowledge-based firms use technology for automation, production efficiencies, and overall productivity improvement. For example, although Wal-Mart is thought of as a leading retailer, it is also considered a knowledge-based company based on its sophisticated inventory management systems.

Knowledge-based companies have fewer tangible assets, such as inventory, plant, and equipment. Instead, their *intangible* assets—their people, their customers, their reputation, their intellectual capital, their ideas, and their time—are the essence of their value. Just as important, most of these intangibles *do not* appear on your company's balance sheet. But these intangibles emerge from the ideas and concepts that your people create. Think of this—the U.S. trade surplus of intangible intellectual property is growing by $25 billion per year. Countries around the world are trying to mimic Americans' leadership in "creating the equivalent of a world-class idea factory."[1]

Accountants have reached no conclusions about how to account for intangible assets. "Softer" measures, such as customer satisfaction, quality of management, or employee retention, are nonfinancial by nature. If recorded, they would differ from company to company. On the other hand, if a firm identifies key gauges—based on these soft measures—and tracks them for their own internal strategic planning, it would learn a lot about where and how value is created.

You may find that the difference between your firm's book value and market value reflects a rough approximation of your intangibles. Studies have shown that a firm's market value may be up to six times greater than its book value. Generally accepted accounting principles don't place a lot of emphasis on valuing intangible assets. But if you want to see how your people strategies translate to the bottom line, there are measures that you can track consistently.

Our current accounting system, based on the concept of double entry bookkeeping, originated in 14th-century Italy as merchants needed better ways to record profit from trade and commerce. The "modern" era of accounting evolved in the 19th century as economies began to shift from agrarian to industrial. In the early 20th century, the balance sheet was the primary financial statement used by bankers to determine a company's liquidity. The income statement became more valuable in the middle part of the century as more financing was raised through stock offerings. Stock purchasers could understand a firm's earning power better through evaluating the income statement.

The balance sheet, in the meantime, continued to record a company's assets and liabilities, or what it owned and what it owed. Accounting measured the products created and sold along with measuring the useful life of the substantial equipment that produced them. The value of these companies was based on their physical assets—primarily plant and equipment.

Today's balance sheet still records what a company owns and what it owes. But the balance sheet of a *knowledge-based company* appears unimpressive compared to that of a *manufacturing-era company*. Many assets will appear as cash, receivables, and inventory. Some intangibles appear under the category of goodwill, such as the patents or trademarks that have a quantifiable royalty stream. Less quantifiable intangibles tend not to be categorized as goodwill. Firms can choose to voluntarily disclose information about their intangibles as a footnote to their financial statements.

Intangible assets are our newest sources of wealth. They drive most of our firms today. In addition to a company's intellectual property, such as its patents, trademarks, or copyrights, intangibles encompass a variety of other items. They include proprietary processes ranging from software systems to unique distribution channels, from management processes to systematized team approaches to projects. A firm's customers are a source of intangible value and so is the aggregate customer list in some industries. What all of these examples have in common is that they are keys to doing business that are unique to your firm.

As intangibles have grown in importance, our traditional reporting systems have become less effective in communicating meaningful measurements. As a result, companies that are interested in stronger results need to create an internally meaningful set of measurements. You first need to identify what is important to measure. Then you will capture, record, and track these data until you have gathered enough meaningful information so that analysis can begin.

And that brings us back to the people factor—your firm's human capital. The heart of knowledge-based companies is the people who work within them. It's people who generate intellectual property in a company. People cultivate relationships with customers. People generate ideas for unique processes or systems. The productivity of people determines the length of time a product or service goes from concept to reality, from sales concept to a collected receivable. People manage projects and other people. If they do it well, you'll see great results. If they do it poorly, you may have a problem.

The expression *human resources* (HR) replaced *personnel* in the late 20th century. In many cases, the change has been euphemistic—HR executes policies and procedures set by senior management. Most firms do not have human capital strategies. They simply look at people as the responsibility of HR. More progressive companies that not only understand their strongest asset is human capital but take the steps to strengthen that capital and make it more productive will be rewarded by better performance and higher valuations. In these cases, the HR function is much more strategic in focus and less procedural. Firms that understand that we're talking about talent, not labor, will be prepared to invest in that talent to create maximum value.

There is an increasing interest in the subject of human capital. This book addresses it from three perspectives. Part One focuses on the *strategic importance of human capital*. It delves into the human capital hub, showing how the focus of the firm has shifted from plantcentric to peoplecentric. It examines characteristics of the workforce in this early stage of the 21st century, including the impact of generational and transient aspects of workers. It makes a clear assertion about viewing your people as talent—that is, value creators—for your firm.

Part Two explores the *measurement aspects of human capital*. It contains opinions of some leading experts on accounting for human capital. Most of these ideas and thoughts are at the cutting edge of leadership on this topic. It is important that although no regulatory requirements force firms to account for human capital in financial statements, leading-edge firms are increasingly voluntarily disclosing such information.

Part Three investigates *how to develop human potential in the firm*. It emphasizes the importance of recruiting talent and providing an optimal work environment. Included are recommendations for creating your own internal measurement tools that capture, record, and track data related to recruiting and retention practices at your firm. Analyzing these data provides you with valuable information for human capital management and development.

Until recently, much focus has been on the need to develop executive-level talent to increase the value of the firm. With the blurring of hierarchies, value is being developed across all categories and levels of employees. New areas of development, such as quantum psychology, are explored to show the power of what happens when people change their limiting beliefs. The importance of the human/technology interface is examined along with how to manage in a virtual environment.

The idea of expanding human capital management into your leadership activities in the community and the nonprofit world is explored. Leaders play a significant role in the successful outcome of human capital strategies. Unless they start from the top, it will be extremely difficult for your people to embrace and adopt effective human capital practices. Finally, the book concludes with a look at your people as human capital investors in your firm.

Human capital is the central focus of most of your revenue and profit-generating activities. Once you evaluate the connection between productive human capital and performance and profitability, you take away strategies and concrete, practical suggestions for enhancing the value of your people. By doing so, you position your firm to stay ahead of the competition and attract, retain, and motivate top people.

This book is written for people who have responsibility for generating revenue, increasing profitability, or enhancing productivity. Executives and managers throughout the firm will benefit by approaching human capital from a strategic perspective. Each chapter contains several key workplace trends that influence human capital management and development. Chapters end with a summary of key points and several "thinking points," which are issues to explore within your firm.

To keep the experience current and make it interactive, you are invited to visit <www.valuing-people.com>. This Web site has the latest interviews with leading thinkers on human capital, case studies of firms in different industries, and an opportunity to exchange ideas with other leaders who are committed to enhancing the value of their people. As a reader of this book, you are invited to benefit by becoming part of the "Valuing People" community.

# PART ONE

# The Strategic Importance of Human Capital

*This section examines characteristics of the workplace in the early part of the 21st century and documents how firms have shifted from plantcentric to peoplecentric as knowledge-based companies have become more prevalent. Also examined are characteristics of four generations in the workplace and how their different perspectives, values, and mores affect performance. This section identifies the distinction between labor and talent and contends that talent is the human capital driver in knowledge-based firms. It explains the mix of people in the workplace and how salaried employees are no longer the status quo in the firm.*

## CHAPTER 1

# Human Capital Is the Hub

The buzz about human capital is getting louder. Strictly speaking, human capital is defined as the collective skills and knowledge of a firm's workforce. When we think of *capital,* we think of some form of wealth—money or property—that can be used to produce more wealth for the firm. The implication behind *human* capital is that the collective competencies of your workforce can boost your firm's productivity and profitability. The challenge is to make your firm's human capital as efficient and effective as possible for maximum value creation.

> **❝** *Human capital is the collective skills and knowledge of a firm's workforce.* **❞**

Numerous examples spotlight the growing awareness of the role human capital plays. Not too long ago, these examples were found primarily in human resources (HR) trade journals. Today we see coverage in the mainstream business press, suggesting that the "soft stuff" surrounding people issues is actually generating the same hard attention:

- Popular business surveys, such as the Hay Group's annual survey of the Global Most Admired Companies published in *Fortune,* focus on employee-based and customer-based measurements. In 2000, the top-ranked companies were "seriously committed to the human elements that contribute to their success."[1] People-oriented measurements such as retention and career development were key factors that ranked as important in 40 percent of the companies surveyed.

- The Watson Wyatt Human Capital Index measures the impact of a firm's people practices on its overall financial performance. Results of a survey of some 400 U.S.-based and Canadian-based companies reveal that "a significant improvement in 30 key HR practices is associated with a 30 percent increase in market value." The five key areas of focus are recruiting excellence; clear rewards and accountability; a collegial, flexible workplace; communications integrity; and a prudent use of resources.[2]

- Eighty percent of respondents in a recent Accenture survey of some 500 international executives believe that "people issues" have become higher priorities in the past several years.[3]

- David M. Walker, comptroller general of the United States, is on record emphasizing the importance of human capital management of federal employees: "Federal employees should be viewed not as costs to be cut but as assets to be appreciated."[4] Under his leadership, the U.S. General Accounting Office (GAO) is undertaking innovative human capital strategies to revamp the government's bureaucratic policies.

- A new company called My Rich Uncle is connecting top students with investors who are willing to bet on the students' earning potential. Students pay a percentage of their annual income for about ten years after graduation to their investor.[5] Imagine that top-performing students who have not yet had real jobs can create a quasi securitization of their earnings before they start working!

## A Snapshot from the Industrial Economy

Our business environment has evolved from the industrial era of machines and processes to the information age of ideas and concepts. As the business environment has shifted, so has the nature of the worker. To understand where we are today and where we are heading tomorrow, it is helpful to get some historical perspective.

In the industrial era, the manufacturing plant was the hub of a company. All activity revolved around the production of goods in the plants. Manufacturing processes were based on the most efficient way of producing a company's goods. The concept of assembly line production resulted in specialization of the various factory jobs. A person was trained to do his or her job without necessarily knowing how it related to the end product.

When orders were strong, the plant would run additional shifts. If business took a dip, the hours were cut back. These blue-collar workers would come to work, punch in, do their jobs, punch out, and leave the job behind at the end of the day. If there were glaring problems, the worker called in a supervisor. It was not the worker's responsibility to think through the problem and come up with a solution. Henry Ford is attributed with asking, "Why do I get a person when all I need is a pair of hands?" This was the reality of being a worker in the industrial era. People were hired to do, not to think.

During this time, white-collar workers progressed in the organization based on performance and unspoken quotas for position and title. This structure was personified in the late William H. Whyte's classic, *The Organization Man.* The paradigm for success was work hard, be loyal, and the company will take care of you. The individual surrendered his or her personality and creativity for the greater good of the corporate goals.

As the service economy evolved toward the end of the 20th century, heavy manufacturing started to fade into the background as the service enterprises of the postindustrial economy emerged. Financial services, computer services, and the entertainment industry are examples of postindustrial enterprises that arose.

Enter the information and knowledge economy. The products and services of most businesses and organizations in this era are based on ideas and concepts. Software companies, pharmaceutical companies, biotechnology firms—all of these firms are based on the generation of intellectual capital, which creates a firm's profits. *People* create that intellectual capital and thus profits.

## $W$ORKPLACE TREND

*The intellectual property of the 21st-century firm is based on ideas and concepts, not machines and processes.*

The hub has shifted from the factory to the people. This doesn't mean that an industrial giant of the 1950s can't be successful today. On the contrary, companies that demonstrate the greatest staying power

**FIGURE 1.1**    Comparison of Companies Comprising the Dow 30

| *October 1, 1928* | *November 1, 1999* |
| --- | --- |
| Allied Chemical & Dye | Alcoa |
| American Can | Allied Signal |
| American Smelting | American Express |
| Atlantic Refining | AT&T |
| American Sugar | Boeing |
| American Tobacco | Caterpillar |
| Bethlehem Steel | Citigroup |
| Chrysler | Coca-Cola |
| General Electric | DuPont |
| General Motors | Eastman Kodak |
| General Railway Signal | Exxon |
| Goodrich | General Electric |
| International Harvester | General Motors |
| International Nickel | Hewlett-Packard |
| Mack Trucks | Home Depot |
| Nash Motors | IBM |
| North American | Intel |
| Paramount Publix | International Paper |
| Postum Inc. | Johnson & Johnson |
| Radio Corp. | McDonald's |
| Sears Roebuck | Merck |
| Standard Oil (N.J.) | Microsoft |
| Texas Corp. | Minnesota Mining (3M) |
| Texas Gulf Sulphur | J. P. Morgan |
| Union Carbide | Philip Morris |
| U.S. Steel | Procter & Gamble |
| Victor Talking Machine | SBC Communications |
| Western Electric | United Technologies |
| Woolworth | Wal-Mart Stores |
| Wright Aeronautical | Walt Disney |

Source: Adapted from the *Wall Street Journal,* 27 Oct. 1999, C15.

have reinvented themselves as information age companies. In fact, the 30 companies that comprise the Dow Jones Industrial Average demonstrate this evolution; the only remnant of a former age is the word *industrial* in the name of this famous index (see Figure 1.1).

## The Human Asset Paradox

From an accounting perspective, an asset is something owned that has an agreed-on trading or exchange value. It is fairly easy to identify when looking at such categories as cash, accounts receivable, inventory, plant and equipment, and so on. But the fundamental flaw in evaluating a human asset is that this asset is not now—nor will it ever be—owned by a firm. So we are quick to say that "people are our greatest assets," but the word *assets* is actually a significant misnomer. We don't own our people. But unfortunately we sometimes treat them as if we do without regard to their intrinsic value.

### *O*NE SIZE DOESN'T FIT ALL

**The Human Asset Paradox**

*Assets are something we own that have an agreed-on trading or exchange value. Human assets can never be owned. People are, in effect, leased to their employers for the duration of their employment. Their value fluctuates based on three factors:*

*1. Whether they work in a job that maximizes their potential*

*2. Whether anything is influencing their productivity (such as hopes of a promotion or dealing with personal problems)*

*3. The market demand for their competencies*

The expression *wage slave* came into popular use in the last decades of the 20th century. People referred to themselves as wage slaves when they worked in jobs where they were not valued for their intrinsic capabilities and potential. When placed into a job without the expectation of professional or personal fulfillment, they tended to think of themselves as "slaves" to the organization—the antithesis of developing human capital.

A person's value as a human asset stems directly from how his or her knowledge, experience, skills, and competencies match the job in which that person works. If we match the right person with the right job, then we fulfill that person's potential. If there is a mismatch, however, we will never stimulate that person's capacity to its fullest. Be honest with yourself as you answer this question: Have you consistently matched the right people into the right jobs so that you can activate their highest potential?

> **❝** *A person's value as a human asset stems directly from how his or her knowledge, experience, skills, and competencies match the job in which that person works.* **❞**

Performers provide a good frame of reference for the contention about a person's value. Michael Jordan is a tremendous human asset when he plays basketball. When he played baseball, his value as a human asset wasn't as high. Midori is a brilliant classical violinist whose value may not be achieved if she played jazz trumpet. Warren Buffett, a genius in long-term value investing, would not be so effective as a day trader in technology stocks.

A person's value as a human asset is dynamic. It doesn't end once he or she is hired into a new position. We need to understand the importance of this mercurial quality. If a person's value becomes static, the unfortunate consequence is that the person will not be activating his or her highest potential. Because a static person doesn't think and create the same way that a growing person does, we see another piece of the paradox: The differences in how people develop potentially affects how they contribute value to the firm.

Companies that are reticent to invest in training and development for all levels of its people will find themselves with an outdated workforce in fairly short order. One of the big objections to an investment in training is that a workforce is mobile—What if I train my people and they leave and take that knowledge elsewhere? The truth is that the necessity for training is a fact of corporate life today. If you don't make the training investment, your people are going to leave anyway. And your firm will suffer unrealized potential profits by *not* having invested in the training.

Your people, however, have the responsibility to take this new knowledge and apply it to their best ability. Each person will respond differently to training, based on his or her knowledge, skills, and experiences. One of the things we can do is to make sure that we match the right training with the right people. Many companies put entire departments of people through exactly the same training when a selective approach would have been better for everyone involved.

By their nature, human assets are talent, not labor. Labor can be trained to perform a task on a repetitive basis without using its brain for output. Talent, on the other hand, implies a natural ability that can be enhanced by being exposed to the right combination of experience and education. Viewing our people as talent rather than labor is a major shift in mind-set. The sooner we understand that we are cultivating talent, we can be completely prepared to invest in our people.

> **❝** *Talent implies a natural ability that is enhanced by the right combination of experience and education.* **❞**

Another aspect of the paradox that human asset value fluctuates is that people are sentient beings. When they are on top of the world and feeling good about their contributions, they are unstoppable. On the other hand, if they are distracted for whatever reason, their productivity will diminish and over time will have a negative impact. If you hire correctly, employee self-esteem won't be an issue. But when people suffer from serious personal problems, they are likely to perform below their normal ability. In fact, after the terrorist attacks on the World Trade Center and the Pentagon on September 11, 2001, many companies experienced productivity drops as people processed their fears. You can't specifically plan for disasters that increase employees' personal problems, but if you are caught unprepared, the outcome can be damaging for your firm.

So this paradox of fluctuating human asset value *is* complex. Think of your firm's human capital as a form of wealth that will create more wealth. Under routine circumstances, this will be true—as long as you bear in mind that you can't turn a quarterback into a linebacker. The objective is to create productive capital from your unique human assets.

> **❝** *Your firm's human capital is a form of wealth that will create more wealth.* **❞**

## Human Capital = Value Creation

This discussion can be synthesized to a fairly simple premise: Treat your people well and they will treat you well. Simple to say, difficult to implement. Focus on the productivity of the factory worker required an entirely different mind-set. There the worker was evaluated on output per shift. Today the worker is ultimately evaluated on the basis of the value he or she creates for your business. It is always in your best interest to create the optimal environment for your people. By doing so, you can generate the best results from your human assets—whom you don't own nor have a claim to—so that your firm can prosper.

## *W*ORKPLACE TREND

*Firms that understand the correlation between human capital and value creation are competitively positioned for the future.*

If you believe that by enhancing the value of your people you enhance the value of your firm, you already possess the mind-set. If you don't believe this, then you may have some soul searching to do about what it will take to bring your firm to the next level. You may think that the answer is technology or automation, but technological savvy and automatism come from human assets. You are still faced with issues of human capital management.

**66** *When you enhance the value of your people, you enhance the value of your firm.* **99**

Remember that you choose your firm's priorities, so you can choose to adopt or reject a mind-set that values human capital. There may be days when you feel as though you "didn't accomplish a thing" because you spent your entire day on people issues. Chances are, your day *was* productive—you just don't see tangible results yet. As managers move up the line, they spend more time on people issues. If you understand the connection between the investment of your time and ultimate value creation, you will look at your daily responsibilities and accomplishments from a more assured perspective.

Value created by your people can be measured. We can identify a relationship between investments in training and incentive-based compensation, for example, and performance. When companies hire the best people for the job and provide an environment receptive to employee development, they will experience higher levels of retention. The cost of replacing people is so high that increased retention has a direct effect on your bottom line. Firms that quantify these nonfinancial measures and act on the information will ultimately be more profitable. These topics will be explored in more detail in Chapters 4 and 5.

## $W$*ORKPLACE TREND*

*Increasingly, companies are attaching nonfinancial measures to their processes to track and analyze performance in more quantifiable ways.*

## Spokes of the Human Capital Hub

**FIGURE 1.2**    The Human Capital Hub

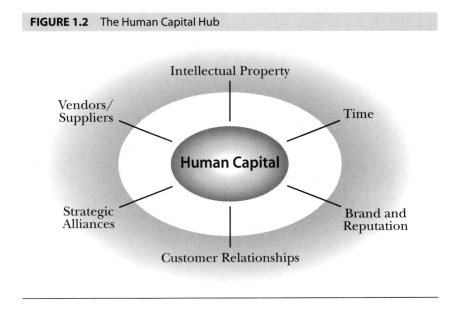

Now that you know that enhancing human capital enhances value creation, let's look at the spokes of this human capital hub and see how the interconnected whole makes up the intrinsic value of the firm (see Figure 1.2).

### Intellectual Property

People create ideas that result in marketable products and services. Some of these are proprietary and can be trademarked or patented. In the knowledge economy, there has been a shift in what firms deem appropriate for intellectual property protection. Historically, something generated from a company's research and development would be eligible for protection. Today, however, there has been an enormous increase in the application for trademarks and patents. The difference is that firms are taking anything that can potentially represent a marketing advantage and are applying for protection. Even ideas can be trademarked today, not just new products. A "business method" can be protected as long as the idea produces a useful result,[6] which represents a huge shift from even a decade ago.

In many cases, however, the ideas and processes that comprise your firm's intellectual property may not be trade secrets. Instead, they may represent the specific manner and nuances of how your people execute your work. It may be a nonexclusive process that is repeated consistently and with excellence so that customers *perceive* it as unique. This type of intellectual property is as important as anything you may submit for trademark protection.

One of the key elements of the successful generation of intellectual property is a corporate culture that permits making mistakes. People who are afraid to make mistakes are not likely candidates for risking their creative juices on the job. Think of the legendary story of Thomas Edison, who had thousands of failed attempts before he perfected electric light. Talent wants to innovate and experiment. Labor wants to cover its backside. You can't have the originality of talent without potential backfires.

Sometimes intellectual property can arise from mistakes. Consider the famed story of the engineer at 3M who was conducting experiments to produce a new adhesive. The outcome of these experiments was not going as planned. Some of the "inadequate" adhesive stuck to the back of some paper on his desk. He tacked up the note and by accident discovered that even after removing the stuck paper from his desk, he was still able to readhere it elsewhere. One thing led to another and Post-it notes were born. What is important is that the learning environment at 3M permitted—and even encouraged—mistakes. As a result, the 3M engineer's desire to succeed was not suppressed by a fear of failing when he developed Post-its.

Other intellectual capital is created from knowledge sharing. Firms that have a high value of trust are primed for knowledge sharing to be a successful tactic. Encouraging knowledge sharing in a nonhierarchical way benefits the firm because people feel free—and trusting—to share what they know with their colleagues. A number of global companies have intranets where employees post information. Employees can ask questions, work out problems, or simply post information that helped them in a particular way. This stimulates creativity in a way entirely different from more traditional brainstorming.

## Customer Relationships

The way your people interact with your customers is another vital spoke on the human capital hub. The old adage that people do business with those they like and trust has become more important in the information age. Cultivation of these relationships is often the distinguishing feature that converts a prospect to a customer—especially in this increasingly commodity-focused and impersonal business environment.

A number of companies espouse the philosophy that the customer comes first, or the customer is always right. Those who believe this to the detriment of their people will lose in the long run. If you start with your people—and treat them right—they will treat the customers the way they are treated. It is a way to demonstrate to them that you know customer relationships start with them.

**❝** *If you treat your people well, they will treat customers the way they are treated.* **❞**

Many companies separate their sales and customer service functions. Although there is usually a sound reason to do so, wherever possible create the concept of a relationship manager, who is the point person within your company for the client. Relationship managers guide clients through the complexity characteristic of so many large firms today. In recent years, that complexity has evolved into sophisticated software applications that allow companies to more accurately track pertinent information about clients. Relationship management became a buzzword in the 1990s, but it has existed in the form of customer servicing for a long time. If you train your people to be relationship managers, their mind-set will gravitate toward answering the question, "How can I best serve my customers?"

Observe the unique ways your people interact with their customers. Notice how they cultivate and enhance these relationships over time. It is important to remember that this interaction takes place at all levels of a company. In fact, in the retail and hospitality sectors, the lowest-paid employees interface most frequently with customers. If these employees feel appreciated in their job, they will go the extra mile with customers.

Have you asked your people how their job can be done better or more efficiently? More important, have you asked in a way that makes them comfortable in giving you sincere recommendations? Some of the best suggestions for improvement come from your lowest-level people. If they feel valued in the work they do, they will reward you with sincere, constructive feedback and feel compelled to do an even better job. Engage your people as you would engage a client. Countless examples indicate how workers feel substantially more appreciated when they are given *carte blanche* to make suggestions for improvement.

## Vendors and Strategic Alliances

Until recently, dealings with vendors and suppliers were not perceived as priority relationships. After all, you are in the customer role with your vendors. In the human capital hub, however, our relationships with vendors and suppliers can flourish. Where there is a long-term mutually beneficial affiliation, these relationships can "morph" into strategic alliances. You don't just buy from your vendor; you have a symbiotic relationship where what is good for one party is good for the other.

These alliances may not develop with all relationships, but think about the long-term advantages of treating these relationships as you would treat your client relationships. You can each be a resource for the other. You may introduce each other to potential business referrals. Or a day may come when you are suffering financial difficulty, and vendor relationships could make the difference between shutting your door and staying in business.

A thriving agency business accepted bad advice from an incompetent financial advisor, ending up with severe cash flow problems and on the verge of filing for bankruptcy. The agency owner called on all of the firm's vendors in person. She told them the truth about the firm's situation and proposed a payment plan. Because of the good, ten-plus-year relationships that the company had developed with these vendors, it stayed afloat and survived. This could have easily ended in bankruptcy and the vendors would have received their ten cents on the dollar. Instead, they worked together and came up with a solution that worked for everyone. This is the difference between having a relationship with vendors/suppliers and merely performing transactions.

## Time

In the manufacturing era, productivity was measured by the output created in a given fixed period. Assembly lines were paced so that a certain amount of inventory was produced in a given shift. Workers were expected to perform so that these quotas were met. There was no such thing as "having a bad day"—it was still your responsibility to do what you were being paid to do. If you didn't do your job, your pay was docked. Time cards were kept on most employees, blue-collar and white-collar alike. Your paycheck was based solely on your hourly wage times the number of actual hours you worked in a given period.

Time is the inventory of knowledge workers. Time limits our ability to generate ideas and concepts. And people not only control their time but they control their output. There is no longer a real need for the 9-to-5 shift as we knew it in the manufacturing era. Even though companies have evolved to using flextime and telecommuting more frequently, most companies still rely on the industrial concept of a fixed eight-hour day, Monday through Friday.

Under this scenario, a manager may be able to control how much time a person spends in the office but cannot control a person's creative and intellectual output during that same period. As a result, time has really become the knowledge economy worker's inventory. A lot of traditional thinking breaks down when we examine time in this manner. For example, a person's most important idea may not be created while on the job—it could emerge in the car while commuting, while watching his child's soccer match, or while attending a concert. But he is still expected to show up between 9 and 5, five days a week.

Ironically, time lost its linearity with the emergence of the 24-hours-a-day, 7-days-a-week (24/7) world of the Internet. As a result of time compression, people began to operate in "simultaneous time," where the past, present, and future converge.[7] If your customers expect a 24/7 level of responsiveness, then you need to comply. But if your company still operates under an industrial era concept of working 9 to 5, you will be hard-pressed to satisfy your customers.

Workers are expected to give their coworkers and customers 24/7 treatment without regard to its long-term physical, mental, and emotional impact. Surveys and stories have revealed that many people consistently do some business-related e-mail or voice mail from home in the evening because, they say, they have no choice. They fear they will not be able to keep up with what is expected of them on the job if they don't supplement their work time at home.

One of the consequences is a considerable blurring of the physical boundaries between home and business life. Many people have a home office, but even if they don't have a dedicated office per se, they tend to have an area used for working on their laptops at home. A big issue is how to maintain personal boundaries when physical boundaries have broken down.

From a human capital perspective, it is fair to say that the combination of time compression and blurring of work-life boundaries means that companies are getting more work out of their people than what is perceived on the surface in the 9-to-5 world. When people feel valued, they will work extra hours willingly and gladly. When they don't feel valued, they work extra hours with resentment and disgust. Either way, these feelings have a carryover effect, whether positive or negative.

> 66 *When people feel valued, they will work extra hours willingly. When they don't feel valued, they work extra hours with resentment.* 99

## Your Firm's Brand or Reputation

Your reputation is typically based on one or more strong corporate values that are consistently reinforced by human capital activities. If the company is visible and well known, that reputation may be represented by a brand, such as McDonald's or Coca-Cola. McDonald's was built around Ray Kroc's values of "Quality, Service, Cleanliness, and Value." The Coke brand, as American as apple pie, was built around a distinctive curvy bottle and an image of enjoying life. Consider these examples where the people factor makes a difference in the image:

- Wal-Mart is known as a low-priced retailer, and the greeters who welcome customers into the store enhance its reputation. It's pleasant to shop at Wal-Mart.

- Southwest Airlines has a reputation for having fun. The people who work there have fun and so do their passengers.

- At Home Depot, customers can ask the associates anything about projects they are working on and will get cheerful, helpful advice.

- Lands' End operators gladly take orders, answer questions, and offer friendly chitchat to customers.

- Dell tech support people ask the right questions and don't make you feel like you don't know what you're doing (even if that happens to be the case).

For firms that don't enjoy this sort of high visibility, however, your reputation is derived from the same things—your corporate values and the human capital activities that support them. Local businesses across the country do this as well as their larger counterparts.

The key to success in developing your reputation has two components. First is the strong articulation of your corporate values. Are they more than words on a piece of paper—would employees in all areas of your company know what you stand for? This is where one of the big "disconnects" takes place. Corporate executives think that they have effectively communicated a wordy mission statement to their people. The trouble is that if the mission statement is hard to understand or buried in a policy manual, people can't be expected to remember. Southwest Airlines, for example, communicates its mission, vision, and values throughout the company to remind its workers what is important and what makes Southwest a great company.

The second component, of course, is fostering human capital activities that support your values. If you say that one of your values is "caring" and your people feel they are treated badly, this value will never be carried over to your reputation. Say what you mean and then "walk your talk." Plenty of smaller firms have developed excellent reputations in their industries and successfully compete against the Goliaths of their fields. Their reputation precedes them—and they walk their talk.

## Make Human Capital a Strategic Initiative

The reality is that the people who spawn your income-producing ideas walk away from their desks every night and out of your building. As we've seen in the human capital hub, they are involved at all levels of the value chain that produces the product or service that brings in revenue for your firm.

You may think you have your employees under control. You may have a highly competent HR department that oversees your people processes. That may be true, but is your head of HR a strategic member of your executive team? More significant, is he or she a key strategic ally of the CEO? General corporate practices indicate that the head of HR may be in an executive role but rarely in a strategic one. Furthermore, it is the rare CEO who emerges from the HR function. So, there is room for change in perceptions as well as activities.

Two key strategic imperatives must be considered: human capital management and human capital development. Consider forming a human capital strategy team consisting of the head of HR, the CFO, and the head of strategic planning. The CEO should be well informed if not an ad hoc member of this team. Start by creating a human capital strategic plan to identify your talent needs in the next three to five years. Then, perform a human capital audit to determine where shortfalls exist. Your human capital audit may reveal gaps in a variety of areas. See the Appendix for a sample human capital audit.

## Possible Reasons for Human Capital Shortfalls

A key reason why companies fall short in their human capital initiatives tends to be that they don't invest the time and resources to make it a key strategic initiative. Many still view people as labor and expense rather than as an investment in talent. Firms that are hierarchically structured may not be inclusive in sharing corporate values and mission across the ranks. Furthermore, most firms don't take the time to create the measurements that can help them truly understand the impact of their investment in people, whether it is training, compensation, leadership, or creativity.

**Lack of understanding of corporate values and mission.** When people don't understand your company's values and mission, they can inadvertently prevent the company from moving forward. This is a top-down initiative. Your managers need to convey your company's philosophy to their people in meaningful ways. If your employees don't understand corporate values, it may not be their fault. It may be the consequence of inadequate information filtering down from a higher level.

Don't assume that your people memorize your employee handbook and assimilate corporate values from reading. Mission and values need to go beyond words—they need to be integrated into the way you do business. People should be clear about what you stand for from their first encounter with you.

**Insufficient training to support the growth of your people.** Here is something to consider: If you hesitate to pay for training, then you are thinking with an old economy mind-set. In manufacturing's heyday, when people represented costs, training was also a cost. Today, that model doesn't work. Today, your people are your capital—something of value—and training is an additional investment. That's it in a nutshell. The better your people are trained, the better they will perform.

Moreover, there is increasing evidence that investments in training result in stronger performance and ultimately in higher share price. Do a little snooping and find out what other companies like yours are doing in the area of education and training. And make sure that you select the right kind of training that will bring out your people's highest potential. (We'll take a closer look at this in Chapter 4.)

**Inadequate matching of the right person to the right position.** The trap is accepting policies and practices because you've always done things a certain way. Any time such complacency motivates you, consider it a trigger to make substantial changes. A consultant who works in the retail sector performed in-depth assessments for a client. One person who had consistently weak performance appraisals was transferred from a sales position on the floor to a technical position in information technology (IT). In less than a few months, this person discovered and implemented a technical change that yielded over $1 million annually to the retailer. If this person had been kept on the sales floor because "they always did it that way" or been fired without the client's knowing his real calling, a significant loss in profits could have resulted for this company. The topic of matching people to positions will be covered in more depth in Chapter 6.

**Territorialism and politics.** This obstacle sometimes occurs in multidivisional and multidepartmental companies. Employees become territorial because they bet on one particular faction to become the entity in power. Or they align themselves with particular leaders they think will be the rising stars within the company. In either case, human capital suffers because people decisions aren't based on the best strategy for the company.

Politics can also come into play if managers suppress the performance of some of their people by not developing them in their position. Sometimes managers are threatened by an employee's competence and will push the person aside because of the managers' insecurities. Such employees will either burn out or leave after working for these managers for a while. You could lose some of your best people through these types of politics.

**Promotion of your best performers into managers with no coaching, training, or support in their new role.** This is a classic problem. You promote your best salesperson to sales manager. As a great salesperson, she didn't need to be competent in assessing and developing people. To become a great sales manager, however, she needs that competency. If she doesn't receive the training and coaching to assess and develop people, she is set up to fail in her new job as manager.

This is not to say that strong performers can't be promoted into management positions. But when you make this kind of promotion, assess the person's competency in managerial responsibilities. Then you'll know from the start whether the person has the ability and potential or should not be moved into the job.

**People cutbacks to make budget.** Managers who have budget responsibility and the authority to hire and fire can often hide weak operational results behind layoffs. They think that laying off staff will help their numbers. That may be the case in the short term but definitely has the potential to backfire as the company moves forward. There is no question that cutting back staff just to make the numbers work is not only a bad strategy but may also be a sign that the manager is either lazy or panicking.

The antidote is to create nonfinancial measures, such as the ones to be discussed in Chapter 4. By recording and analyzing nonfinancial data, you can identify the real issues precluding financial success. Sometimes you have no choice but to lay off people, but often nonfinancial measurements will shed light on operational issues early enough so that they can be remedied in ways other than cutting staff.

**Motivating people with fear.** This is a holdover from a management tactic that was frequently seen in the manufacturing era: "If you don't produce $x$ amount by $y$ date, then you're on probation." Fear tactics will motivate the weak, who truly dread losing their job. But the strategy is mean-spirited and the antithesis of developing and investing in human capital.

People's fear of losing their job is often irrational but it is a very real fear that tends to be worse during times of economic duress. People are inclined to shut down or play it safe during these times. An increase in cautious behavior, or "playing by the book," is a sign that fear is occurring. A strong human capital management strategy calls for keeping the lines of communication wide open. If there is a legitimate possibility of job losses, the firm that values its people will take steps to ensure that the people who are being let go are given resources and dignity to make as smooth a transition as possible.

**Weakness in critical-thinking skills.** Many people enter the workplace with weak critical-thinking skills. This can be a difficult problem in all types of companies, but particularly in those that are knowledge based and have a need to extrapolate from one idea or process to another. You can help your people develop their critical-thinking skills by giving them room to experiment (and perhaps make mistakes as a consequence).

Sometimes people's critical-thinking skills are dormant because they haven't been in an employment situation that activates critical thinking. Give your people the tools and coaching to improve in this area. The competency of critical thinking is increasingly important in today's companies, and deficiencies might slow down your company's progress.

**Inadequate technology skills.** Today, everyone needs to know at least a little about technology. As technology affects more of our systems and processes, we need to interface with it on some level. Whether it is learning a new customer relationship management (CRM) software or simply retrieving e-mail, people need a minimum level of skill to be effective.

Technology can usually be taught unless a person resists. Technophobia is not age driven. It's a mind-set. If you have people who aren't willing to get comfortable with at least the minimum level of technology that your firm uses, then you have a mismatch. As long as employees are open-minded and willing to learn, on the other hand, technology skills can be learned.

## Final Thoughts

It is important that your executive team has a unified mind-set about the importance of human capital management and development. This should not become a politicized issue within your organization. Human capital management is the ultimate win-win scenario. By bringing out the best in your people, your firm will benefit. Equally important, the people themselves will benefit from the opportunity to be value creators for your company. The strategy, then, serves the best interests of the firm as well as the individual.

## CHAPTER RECAP

### Workplace Trends

- The intellectual property of the 21st-century firm is based on ideas and concepts, not machines and processes.

- Firms that understand the correlation between human capital and value creation are competitively positioned for the future.

- Increasingly, companies are attaching nonfinancial measures to their processes to track and analyze performance in more quantifiable ways.

### Summary of Key Ideas

- Human capital is the collective skills and knowledge of a firm's workforce.

- A person's value as a human asset stems directly from how his or her knowledge, experience, skills, and competencies match the job in which that person works.

- Talent implies a natural ability that is enhanced by the right combination of experience and education.

- Your firm's human capital is a form of wealth that will create more wealth.

- When you enhance the value of your people, you will enhance the value of your firm.

- The human capital hub shows people at the center of the activity of the knowledge-based firm. Intellectual property and ideas, time, vendors, strategic alliances, customer relationships, and the firm's reputation are spokes emanating from this hub.

- If you treat your people well, they will treat customers the way they are treated.

- When people feel valued, they will work extra hours willingly. When they don't feel valued, they work extra hours with resentment.

## Thinking Points

- Create a human capital strategy team to assess your firm's strengths and weaknesses and recommend ways to improve.

- Think about how your firm aligns its values and mission with its human capital strategy. How can you achieve more continuity in this area?

- Does your corporate culture allow for mistakes? Think about what you can do to give employees the opportunity to take more risks.

- How is your company sensitive to your people's boundaries between work and home?

- Review the section on making human capital a strategic initiative and identify areas of improvement for your company.

## CHAPTER 2

# Bridging the Generations

We are living in an unprecedented moment in the history of work. The beginning of the 21st century marks the first time that four generations are concurrently employed. These generations are bound largely by their values and mind-sets. Each generation has distinctive views of what employment means to it. While a generation is based on the years in which its members were born, generations are connected through life experiences shared as their members grow up. They share popular culture, current news events, music, heroes, and a work ethic.

## WORKPLACE TREND

*For the first time in history, four generations are concurrently found in the workplace.*

Our world of work represents a life experience that all generations share. Although our individual perspectives are based largely on the shared experience of our generational peers, our attitude is also affected by people not of our generation. We learn from people of all generations, older and younger. Our mentors can affect our point of view as much as do our peers.

Understanding generational dynamics is an important human capital strategy. People who are more attuned to others' perspectives work better together, which leads to enhanced productivity. Coworkers who enjoy mutual respect have the foundation on which to build the trust that can result in more collaborative and effective work.

# Psychographic Overview

Understanding the individual dynamics and the interrelationships of generations helps us become more effective managers of human capital. It is important to understand that generational descriptions are broad generalizations, including some stereotypes. We need to get to know and understand our people as *individuals* within the context of their generation.[1]

## Matures

Matures (also known as the World War II or silent generation) were born between the beginning of the 20th century and the end of World War II (1945). As this generation spans 40 to 50 years, some of its characteristics may be more relevant for older members while others are more pertinent to younger members. Having experienced both the depression and World War II, they tend to be hard workers who wanted to provide a better future for their children. Self-sacrifice is a virtue for this generation. They embrace the value of teamwork and have tremendous respect for authority.

Having overcome monumental obstacles, matures prospered and were the first beneficiaries of middle-class success in manufacturing-era America. Financial discipline and the Golden Rule were key values that strengthened as this generation aged. Many have strong loyalty to "buying American" and buy traditional products. Successful matures are comfortable spending money but avoid lavish and extravagant purchases.

**66** *Matures were the first beneficiaries of middle-class success in manufacturing-era America.* **99**

## Baby Boomers

More than 71 million baby boomers were born between 1946 and 1964. It is significant that more births occurred between 1948 and 1953 than in the prior 30 years combined. This huge population concentration was the beginning of a boom that has been consequential on many levels. For example, in the 1960s, more people went to college than ever before. The older boomers, in particular, were strongly influenced by events of the sixties. The civil rights and women's movements gathered momentum. The hippie subculture emerged as did wider access to birth control. The Vietnam War escalated in the 1960s, resulting in a philosophical split among its constituency. In the late sixties, boomers started to vote and have been a tremendous electoral influence ever since.

Boomers were shaped by their parents' strong middle-class aspirations and the postwar economic prosperity that began in the 1950s. Often characterized as the "me" generation, they embrace products and services that make their life easier and less complicated. They have been tremendous spenders and consumers, and were the first generation to be influenced by television as children. They have been rule-breakers and nonconformists, and see themselves as stars of the show. They believe they are in control and invincible on many levels. This invincibility was shaken by the terrorist attacks on the World Trade Center and Pentagon on September 11, 2001, events that marked the first time in the boomers' lifetime that they weren't able to automatically take things for granted.

Boomers have become the most stressed-out generation, largely as a result of their focus on work and consequent overload of decisions and responsibilities. Many strive for simplicity as an antidote to stress. They do not view themselves as old and see middle age as merely a chronological concept, not a mind-set. Boomers feel they will become middle aged at some point in their 70s.

This generation will be the first to reinvent retirement. Because of their carefree spending habits, boomers don't have the nest eggs that their parents had. As a result, many will need to continue working later in life. Regardless of their financial requirements, they will still be vital members of the workforce in their later years although in less traditional jobs than the typical 9-to-5 corporate scenario.

**66** *Boomers will be the first generation to reinvent retirement as we know it.* **99**

Boomers spend money on anything that makes their life easier as well as on material things that commemorate their success. Many suffer from large amounts of personal debt, as they have aspired to a certain quality of life. Insufficient earnings have not been enough reason for boomers to forgo their desires and lifestyle dreams.

## Generation X

Members of Generation X, or Gen Xers, (also known as the baby bust or lost generation) consist of some 46 million people born between 1965 and 1979. Gen Xers came of age as the economic prosperity of the prior three decades retracted in the 1980s. The oldest Gen Xers entered the workforce at a time of full employment in the economy. In effect, the younger boomers soaked up much of the inventory of good jobs, leaving Gen Xers with career challenges. Many college graduates entered the workforce by taking administrative or clerical jobs, because those were the only ones available to them.

Gen Xers grew up suspicious of the values of the boomers and often question anything that smacks of the status quo. In contrast to their boomer elders, for example, Gen Xers don't believe they will receive any money from Social Security. They feel that they will need to be responsible for funding anything that relates to their retirement. Because they entered the workforce at such a precarious time, they do not view corporate America as paternalistic.

Gen Xers are uncertain about life in general and more specifically about their place in the world. According to a poll in 1999, many Gen Xers feel that their parents' divorce was the single most defining event in their life. More Gen Xers grew up with two parents in separate households than had any prior generation. The new economy appeared on the scene as a possible vehicle for defining themselves.[2] By becoming proficient knowledge workers, they felt they would be able to distinguish themselves from boomers and matures.

Gen Xers accept alternative lifestyles and are more comfortable with diversity than are boomers or matures. They concurrently embrace and distrust technology. They work hard yet strive for a balanced life. Their spending habits reflect their interest in achieving this balance, particularly if they are spending for something that can give them immediate gratification. In spite of this, they have tended to be a generation of savers (partly as a reaction to the boomer legacy).

**❝** *Gen Xers concurrently embrace and distrust technology.* **❞**

## Generation Y

Finally, members of Generation Y, or Gen Yers, (also known as the Echo Boom, the Net Generation, or Millennials) were born from 1979 to the late 1990s and currently total around 80 million.[3] They are primarily children of the baby boomers and have more in common with their parents' generation than with their Gen X predecessors. Gen Y teenagers are savvy consumers. Boomers may have been the first generation to grow up in front of the television, but Gen Y is the first generation to grow up as a specific market segment. Advertising targeted directly to this group exceeds $2 billion, 20 times more than the amount spent a decade ago.[4]

**66** *Gen Y is the first generation to grow up as a specific market segment.* **99**

Gen Yers are technologically astute. This is the first time in history when young people have known as much as adults about an innovation that affects society so profoundly, namely the Internet.[5] Many have been exposed to computers since birth and to the Internet during their formative years. As a result, they have access to more information as youngsters than any previous generation. They are also more "wired" than any previous generation. Many Gen Yers use cell phones and pagers, resulting in unprecedented connection with their parents.

There is anecdotal evidence that Gen Yers may be more interested in community affairs than any generation since the matures, and may be "a more generous, practical and civic-minded group"[6] and thus are fostering strong relationships with their grandparents. Today, most high schools have community service requirements, so service is part of the life of Yers as they grow up. More young people know their grandparents than at any time in history. Closeness between grandparents and grandchildren appears stronger than in previous generations, partially because of grandparents living longer and staying connected by e-mail.

Gen Y is culturally and geographically curious. Members are globally oriented as they grew up during the flourishing of the global economy.[7] Largely as a result of the Internet, they see virtually no geographic boundaries in their world. Before the September 11, 2001, terrorist attacks on the World Trade Center and the Pentagon, their world view did not include war other than the battles they had seen in the movies and the news.

## Organizational Perspectives

Matures rose through the ranks of the hierarchical organizational models that were in place from the 1950s until the mid-1970s. The oldest are retired, and the youngest members are approaching the end of their work life as they enter their retirement years. Boomers came of age as the older manufacturing-era models began to break down and increased competitive pressures challenged corporate America. They are in their peak earning years, fully participating in the workplace. Gen Xers are coming of age professionally in the knowledge economy and will become our corporate and organizational leaders in the next decade.

Each of these generations has a specific frame of reference, and this is key to understanding various human capital issues. For example, matures and older boomers grew up in the manufacturing-era environment described in Chapter 1, in which you slowly progressed through the corporation based on performance and unofficial position and title quotas.

On the other hand, the middle and younger boomers experienced the breakdown of this manufacturing economy as they climbed the corporate ladder. Old regimes dissolved. The age of restructuring entered the corporate world, and mergers, divestitures, consolidations, and reengineering became the norm; one consequence was the elimination of large numbers of people in middle-management roles. For the first time in corporate history, massive layoffs of white-collar workers occurred.

At the same time, increased market competition prevailed on a global basis. Companies did whatever it took to stay ahead of the competition and make their mark, taking unprecedented risks to get ahead. As Wall Street demanded more transparency and accountability, publicly held companies began to manage for the short term to please Wall Street, which was not necessarily the best thing for their long-term future.

By the mid-1980s, women and minorities were increasingly positioned as professionals and managers in the corporate world. Many worked for companies that had been dominated by white male culture and the strength of the old boy network. Hard work and loyalty did not necessarily result in the rewards reaped under the old model. The glass ceiling was hit more than occasionally as these workers tried their best to rise to previously unobtainable levels in the corporate world.

By the time Gen Xers entered the workforce, the manufacturing-era model had broken down to the point where images of traditional managers were the subject of ridicule as "Dilbertism" mocked the old status quo. Often, educated Gen Xers didn't get a great start in corporate jobs because availability was so limited. One consequence was that Gen Xers took a much more entrepreneurial and independent approach to work, which has continued through today. A number of Gen Xers jumped onto the dot-com bandwagon, in part because it represented their first opportunity to grab responsible jobs where they could use their brains.

Although it is too early to comment on Gen Yers, they are shaping up as independent workers who will opt for collaboration and speed over hierarchy and routine. They are likely to choose jobs that do not consume them and will support their lifestyles. They have seen the impact of work on their boomer parents, and they want to have balanced lives.

## Workforce Implications

Each of these generations views employment differently. Clearly this will be an ongoing managerial challenge, particularly as more Gen Yers enter the workforce. Companies that want to instill a strong corporate culture need to factor in these generational perspectives. More often than not, you will be integrating people across generational lines. For example, older workers tend to look for job security while their younger colleagues seek career enrichment and advancement.

> 66 Companies that want to instill a strong corporate culture need to factor in generational perspectives. 99

Although many matures worked for the same company during most of their career, Gen Xers and Gen Yers will change jobs *and* careers frequently throughout their working life. The loyalty demonstrated by the matures has been replaced by the consumerism of younger people, who evaluate job opportunities the way they make other decisions as consumers.[8] Gen Yers, in particular, may identify more with what they buy than what they do.[9]

A key consequence of these shifting employment perspectives is that employers no longer call the shots in the authoritarian way they did in the manufacturing era. In effect, work has taken on qualities more akin to consumerism. People "shop around" for the company that they want to work for. And when they shop, they consider the same attributes—price, quality, convenience, and so on. As a result, power has shifted away from employers to employees, just as power has shifted from producers to consumers.

### *O*NE SIZE DOESN'T FIT ALL

***Workers Have Become Sophisticated Consumers of Companies***

*Work has taken on qualities of consumerism. As a result, organizational power has shifted from the employer to the employee, just as power has shifted from the producer to the consumer. People—especially younger people—shop for jobs the way they shop for consumable products. The company needs to offer a job with specific and individual characteristics that appeal to each person.*

Companies invest a lot of time and energy into creating brands that consumers will recognize and trust. You create a successful brand when you build trusted relationships with your consumers. You can apply the same concept to your people. By establishing a recognizable brand, you will lay the groundwork for a trusted relationship with current and prospective employees. The importance of corporate culture as a recruiting and retention tool is discussed in Chapter 5. For now, however, keep in mind that developing a strong employeecentric brand will go a long way toward establishing your reputation as an "employer of choice."

### *W*ORKPLACE TREND

*Developing a strong employeecentric brand will go a long way toward establishing your reputation as an "employer of choice" in a world where people increasingly "shop" for employment.*

## Managing across the Generations

Companies need to know how to effectively hire and manage across four generations. Each generation has a different work ethic that affects its members' conduct and attitudes toward their job. This issue has important implications for companies in their developing human capital strategies. Your human capital executive and line managers need to be keenly tuned into the expectations and aspirations of all four groups. Again, it is important to emphasize that we can speak generally about the different generations to establish context, but the way that your people relate to these values as individuals is more important. Here are some of the many issues to consider.

## Demographic Implications

The matures are numerically smaller than the boomers and span more than 40 years. They were the only generation in the workforce for most of their working years. When the initial rush of boomers entered the workforce in the late 1960s, the work environment of matures changed immediately and continued on a breathless path until the late 1980s. At this time, the Gen Xers entered the workforce with yet another set of values. For the second time, matures were faced with coworkers whose world view was different from theirs. And it's happening yet again with Gen Yers.

Because Gen X is a comparatively small generation following the wave of boomers, a talent shortage at entry levels and middle levels still exists in many companies. Although this will change as more Gen Yers begin to work, shortages are projected at the other end of the spectrum as boomers reach retirement age. The Bureau of Labor Statistics projects that the gap between available jobs and people available to fill them will reach 6 million by 2008. It projects that this shortage will peak from 2015 to 2025 as boomers reach retirement age.[10]

Managers will face demographic challenges if their workforce corresponds with society at large. Significant numbers of matures and boomers will retire as a smaller proportion of Gen Xers enters middle- and upper-management ranks. Gen Y will swell into the lower ranks, resulting in a younger and less experienced workforce with fewer experienced leaders at the helm.

## Labor versus Talent

This is an important distinction that is perceived differently across generations. Labor was prevalent in the manufacturing era, whereas talent is necessary for knowledge-based companies today. Older workers are less likely to make this distinction between labor and talent. Younger workers *do* make this distinction. Managers who make hiring decisions based on the labor model will be severely disappointed by the outcome. Labor model adherents hire for skills, whereas talent model adherents hire for competencies, which represent a blend of skills, intelligence, attitudes, and behavior.

## $W$ORKPLACE TREND

*Younger people make the distinction between talent and labor and increasingly are adapting the talent mind-set.*

For example, labor model followers hire a technical support person who has good computer skills. Talent model followers hire for the same position but look at what is really necessary to do the best job. Using this example, customer service expertise and interpersonal skills are probably more important than computer skills. So it makes sense to hire a person with strong customer service and interpersonal competencies and then train them with the computer skills necessary to do the best job. Don Tapscott, author and information technology expert, reinforces this point by saying that in the new economy "the means of production shifts to the brain of the producer."[11] That's talent, not labor.

Human capital strategies will be increasingly important as the talent model flourishes. Talent wants to be paid based on performance for the firm. Younger workers will tend to gravitate to firms that recognize their contributions, for example, by using incentive-based compensation or proactive employee development programs. They will be much more likely to move elsewhere if they perceive that their current employers don't value them.

## Organizational Structure

Many older boomers and younger matures are products of the manufacturing-era hierarchies. Those who are in key managerial or leadership positions may retain vestiges of the bureaucratic mind-set so beautifully satirized in the cartoon "Dilbert." They need to be mindful that their people—particularly the younger people—will not stay on the job if they embody the autocratic manager.

Participatory management styles have become the standard, not the exception.

One potential area of disharmony across the generations is the comfort level employees have with hierarchy and bureaucracy versus collaboration and teamwork. Each group views these management styles differently, making them an area ripe for conflict if not handled with all generations in mind. Broadly speaking, matures are the most likely to tolerate hierarchy and structure, mainly because they are accustomed to that type of working environment from the manufacturing era. Boomers don't like hierarchy but deal with it and work around it. Gen Xers are more receptive to teamwork and shun bureaucratic overtures from management. And Gen Yers, frankly, may not comprehend the purpose of bureaucracy; it isn't part of their world view.

The view of organizational structure is one of those areas where the attitudes of the different generations have blended together. Younger workers who are visibly less tolerant of autocratic managerial styles have affected their older colleagues' view. Matures, then, may be more tolerant of structural hierarchies and bureaucracy by virtue of their generational view, but this perspective may be redressed by the influence of their younger coworkers.

## View of Family

In general, matures honor their family relationships. Many grew up surrounded by extended families and continued this tradition with their children, boomers and older Gen Xers. Matures operate from the perspective of middle-class values. Although they can be credited with substantial accomplishments in their own life, they paved the way for their children to have a better life and more opportunities than they did. As a result, their children benefited from higher education and more job opportunities as they entered the workforce. In short, matures lived for their children as they strove to make the world better for them.

Boomers started their adult life influenced by these values, but they were also substantially swayed by the events of the 1960s. The social mores of the sixties affected their attitudes about marriage and family. Younger matures and boomers, for example, are the first people to experience widespread divorce as the norm. Nearly 16 percent of the younger half of boomers have never married. Boomers represent 60 percent of all divorced people in the United States over age 15 and have a higher probability of divorce by the time they retire.[12]

Gen Xers look skeptically at boomers, perceiving they "blew it." As previously mentioned, many Gen Xers feel defined by being children of divorced parents. They have a stronger commitment to family than did their parents. They aspire to have strong families and live in committed marriages. Both Gen Xers and Gen Yers have views about the family unit different from the views of their older colleagues, given their personal experience with divorce. A survey by Yankelovich Partners in 1997 revealed that 73 percent of Gen Xers supported a return to more conventional family standards, up from 1977 when 56 percent of boomers felt this way.[13]

Gen Yers are beginning their adult quest with a strong view about family. In spite of their frequently fractured family structures, they have been close with their parents. Nonfamily issues, such as consumerism and technology, bring them together. Because retailers and manufacturers have specifically targeted Gen Yers, parents of Gen Yers often discuss purchasing decisions with them. They are wired together as well. Pagers and cell phones are becoming standard issue among teens, particularly when both parents work and when so many are divorced. Parents have granted cell phone privileges as a way to be connected with their children when, for various reasons, they are physically separated from them.

## Lifestyle Issues

Younger members of Gen X and Gen Y are concerned about lifestyle issues. They want their work to be meaningful, and they will work for a company as long as they feel they are growing, learning, and contributing. "Paying your dues" is not an assumption for these workers. They want to learn and grow, and have ample opportunity for cultivating leisure activities as well. Their life is not their work.

Matures are reasonably comfortable with their lifestyles, so these are not likely to be a factor in their decision to work for a company. Baby boomers, on the other hand, work hard and want lifestyles that reflect success from that hard work, which is how a lot of boomers got into debt; they appeared to be doing very well financially, but many needed to borrow to make the point.

Some economists and sociologists question whether the search for a balanced life will be important during times of economic uncertainty. It is unlikely that younger people will let economic hardship affect their desire to have work-life balance. They will feel that they have plenty of time to make enough money to live comfortably. Older boomers and matures who have not saved, on the other hand, may feel pressured to forgo lifestyle desires to make up for weaker personal finances.

> 66 *Younger workers want to learn and grow, and have ample opportunity for cultivating leisure activities as well. Their life is not their work.* 99

## Entitlements

The dearth of entry-level talent that preceded Gen Y's coming of age has resulted in a significant increase in attitudes of entitlement. Although these attitudes were exacerbated during the dot-com boon, vestiges still exist. An attitude of entitlement is best characterized by the question, "What's in it for me?" Many younger workers have come to expect various perks and privileges as enticements to work and will not likely relinquish the perks that were customary in the workplace when they started their career.

A lot of these perks are lifestyle driven, ranging from concierge services on the job that provide people to run errands, pick up dry cleaning, or buy birthday gifts, to childcare services that range from on-site day care to charter schools supported by the company. Other services help employees apply for financial aid for their children's college education.

Although some of these perks may seem frivolous and trivial, it still makes sense to include lifestyle-related perks as optional benefits for your people. In the big picture, these are some of the "little things" that give the impression your company understands lifestyle issues and is willing to make lifestyle-related perks available as part of its corporate culture. Increasingly, these lifestyle perks will have an impact on your company's bottom line, as they may make a difference in your ability to retain your best talent.

> 66 *Increasingly, lifestyle perks will have an impact on your company's bottom line, as they may make a difference in your ability to retain your best talent.* 99

## Diversity Issues

Older workers are still more cautious about diversity than are younger people. Matures dominated the workforce when diversity issues gathered more momentum in the late 1960s and early 1970s. From their world view, diversity arrived by government mandate. Women and minorities in the older half of the boomers may have been hired under quotas from the early days of the Equal Employment Opportunity Commission (EEOC).

In the meantime, demographic shifts are occurring in race, religion, ethnicity, and sexual preference. As these converge, we are seeing a different complexion in America that is replicated in the workplace. The rapid growth of the Hispanic population is one example; another is the rise in the number of Muslims in the United States. The number of same-sex couples has increased as well.

Many companies pay lip service to the issue of diversity by declaring it important in their corporate mission statements. Often, however, a significant gap exists between the words on paper and corporate behavior. Companies with a multicultural workforce need to embrace the diversity of their people and offer opportunities for everyone to learn about the "others" and understand more about who they are.

Such understanding is particularly obvious in the higher ranks of companies. From observing corporate America today, it is clear that the percentage of women and minorities in the executive ranks of companies is small. Older minority workers will tolerate the situation until they retire. Younger people who don't feel that they fit in, on the other hand, will find companies that embrace them for who they are. And if they are discouraged by what they find in the corporate world, like prior generations they will opt for free agency or become business owners.

## Communication Issues

It's clear that we need to keep the generational context in mind when we communicate with our colleagues. People react differently to the same action or comment based on their individual behavioral style as well as on their generational perspective. Here's an example. You are extremely pleased with the outcome of a multi-million-dollar project that will generate huge profits for your firm over the next few years. You want to reward your team with a surprise bonus. You give $500 to each of four team members to express your thanks. These are some possible reactions:

- A 60-something worker who has been with the company for ten years is pleasantly surprised to receive the check as she has never received a bonus in the past. She plans to use the money for her grandchild's college fund.

- A team member in his late 40s rolls his eyes when he sees the check. He appreciates the gesture but thinks the amount is pitiful compared with the $500,000 the company is making from *his* idea. He deposits the money in his checking account and will spend it on his upcoming trip to Europe.

- A teammate in his early 30s deposits the check in his bank account. He fully expected to receive a bonus but thinks this one is such a tokenism that he'll just use it to pay bills.

- A worker in her early 20s is stunned there is no acknowledgement given the team as a whole. She's clearly happy to receive the unexpected money but can't imagine why the team as a whole isn't being recognized. Team recognition is as important as her individual award.

Yes, these reactions exemplify the four generations; and it's likely that you've experienced something similar on either the giving or receiving end. It may seem like a lot of extra work to think through communicating to different generations. It boils down to being sensitive about different values—the same way you would to a friend or family member.

## Views of Authority

This is another value that means different things to different generations. Matures are more deferential toward authority. They grew up with this value, and it was reinforced by the World War II culture along with the expectations of the manufacturing-era work environment. Think of the old adage that you should speak only when spoken to—a metaphor for this generation.

Older boomers may be deferential but not necessarily respectful. They willingly follow authority as long as they agree with the course of action. They may work all weekend to complete a project (following authority) but will curse either the company or their manager if they don't agree with the project or respect their manager.

Younger boomers and Gen Xers are suspicious of authority. Not always satisfied with the status quo, they resist authority if they don't trust the person in charge. Their conduct is withdrawn and uninterested rather than a vocal expression of their distrust. Finally, Gen Yers may not understand the full implications of authority, as they view work and life from a more collaborative perspective. Authority may be a curiosity to them that just doesn't make sense.

These perspectives on authority have interesting managerial implications. People who manage across generations need to be mindful of these differences. Older workers may be accustomed to the nuances of managing younger people in an authoritative way to which younger people don't react. On the other hand, increasing numbers of young people manage older workers with more of a collaborative, team-oriented approach. Everyone will need to be sensitized to differences. Progressive firms provide training to enhance these intergenerational encounters. By doing so, you are enhancing the value of your people. Creating awareness of cross-generational views on authority should result in higher retention, which has a positive effect on your company's bottom line.

**❝** *Increasing numbers of young people manage older workers with more of a collaborative, team-oriented approach.* **❞**

## Necessity to Work

A common issue across generations is that most working people *have* to work. In the past, companies could use this to their advantage. For example, during an economic downturn they could "make life miserable," knowing that employment options were limited and that people would sit tight. In more prosperous times, on the other hand, firms have tended to be more generous as an incentive for their people to stay at the firm.

This conduct may have worked under the labor model, but it will not work in the talent model. People will stay with an employer when they have the opportunity to develop their potential. In general, older workers are more security oriented than younger workers. As explored in Chapter 3, however, the concept of free agency is spreading in the workplace, and people are increasingly comfortable with the idea of relying on themselves, not a company.

## Maximizing Value in the Old and the Young

One of the curious phenomena that occurred during the prosperous late 1990s was the common perception that people over 50— or over 40—were "over the hill." *Fortune* magazine published a cover article in 1999 entitled "Finished at Forty," which made all working boomers feel they were being put out to pasture.[14] This perception developed for various reasons. The new economy, with its high level of economic prosperity, created feelings of corporate invincibility. Instead of eliminating younger workers from bloated payrolls, companies felt they no longer needed aging, higher-paid workers. Technology had become increasingly important. Younger people were perceived to be technology gurus, while their older colleagues' expertise was perceived as obsolete. The expense of bringing older workers up to speed wasn't as cost-effective as bringing on younger, lower-paid, but technologically savvy, workers. The result was that the employment pipeline filled up with lower-paid, younger boomers and Gen Xers and pushed aside older workers.

This pushing aside of older workers to make room for younger ones is now resulting in a backlash. New economy prosperity has yielded to new economy realism. As the older boomers begin to retire and Gen Xers enter the higher ranks of the organization, gaps will be apparent. Statistically, far fewer members of Gen X are available to fill the shoes of the retiring boomers. While Gen Yers will be filling entry-level positions in the coming years, they will not be filling positions of retiring boomers. One study projects that between 1998 and 2010 the number of managerial jobs will rise by 21 percent, while the number of people between 35 and 50 will fall by 5 percent.[15]

Such a demographic creates an opportunity for companies to enhance the value of their people. As it is unlikely there will be enough people to meet the demand, companies that demonstrate appreciation for their people will be the winners in this supply and demand contest. Talent will gravitate toward companies that provide the opportunity to enhance their value. So what can companies do to preserve and strengthen their value creation potential in the coming years?

## The New Face of Retirement

Government data reveal that the number of people over 65 who continue to work has grown since the mid-1990s. There are over 1 million more workers over 65 in the labor force than there were in 1985.[16] Successful boomers are retiring early, but the majority of boomers will need to continue working in some capacity. If they are in good health, people who reach 55 will live well into their 80s, and they need money to support themselves in the style to which they have become accustomed. A 1998 survey by the American Association of Retired Persons (AARP) concluded that 80 percent of boomers plan to work at least part-time after they retire.[17]

Retirement is being reinvented. Most versions involve some combination of part-time work or consulting. Consider these examples:

- Companies such as Chevron, Prudential Insurance, and Monsanto are customizing consulting and part-time contracts as a way to keep their top performers engaged.[18]

- The Encore Program at Cigna gives employees the opportunity to take early retirement and return to work as part-time consultants. Cigna limits the number of hours these employees work so there are no conflicts with the firm's pension guidelines.[19]

- DSM, the Dutch chemicals group, worked with its trade unions and created a unique plan whereby it pays workers to leave shift work before they burn out and then provides them with desk jobs in later years.[20]

- Lands' End recruits retirees at the holidays for their seasonal labor crunch. These workers receive perks during the year, such as access to the fitness facilities and a part-time benefits package. The biggest attraction for the workers, though, is their ability to connect with people.[21]

- Bonnie Bell, the teen cosmetics company, has a seniors-only production department. The company has saved over $1 million since it took this previously outsourced department in-house. Deadlines are met consistently and turnover is nonexistent.[22]

## The Gen Y View

Gen Yers enter the workforce thinking they can do anything. Since they were born, their boomer parents have convinced them that they were smart and could have and do anything they wanted. Part of this influence has led to Gen Yers' feeling that they are entitled to meaningful work in a pleasant environment where they can learn and grow. If the organization doesn't provide meaningful work, they will leave and find it elsewhere. They are not troubled about being unemployed. After all, they can continue living with their parents until they find what they're looking for.

Gen Yers may take a project approach to work. For example, they may work for a company for 12 to 18 months and make enough money to let them take an adventure trip hiking in the Himalayas. They may be "samplers," working for companies for short periods before "trying on" another company for size. Employers cannot consider young people disloyal when they work for these short periods.

## Possible Solutions

Consider some of these strategies. Continue to offer workers who are soon to be retirees full benefits in exchange for working part-time. Offer recurring seasonal workers a part-time benefits package. Create the opportunity for older workers to telecommute. Hire retired older workers as consultants, allowing them to lend their expertise to a project that is being handled by inexperienced workers.

Another value creation strategy is to proactively create mentoring opportunities between your part-time quasi retirees and your younger Gen Xers and Gen Yers. This is a compelling proposition, especially if your workforce is becoming increasingly younger and inexperienced. Young people are comfortable with older workers, especially considering the number who have relationships with their own grandparents. This sort of mentoring possibility is unthreatening and a win-win for both groups. A possible bonus is "reverse mentoring," whereby younger people mentor the older workers along the technology learning curve.

Companies that successfully integrate younger, inexperienced employees with older, experienced workers will enhance the work experiences of both constituencies. By so doing, both older and younger workers will feel more valued. Many companies ignore the old and get frustrated with the young. Why not be forward thinking and embrace the two in a way that creates more value for your firm?

## Final Thoughts

Understanding the generational dynamics in your company can provide a greater insight into the different points of view among your employees. When you strive for greater understanding about generational differences, your company will benefit in the long run. Many firms place importance on understanding and embracing the differences among people, whether of gender, race, or sexual preference. Adding generational perspective to this list provides another dimension of understanding. When people feel that they are understood, they feel more valued. Employees who feel more valued typically work harder and more productively as a result.

## CHAPTER RECAP

### Workplace Trends

- For the first time in history, four generations are found concurrently in the workplace.

- Developing a strong employeecentric brand will go a long way toward establishing your reputation as an "employer of choice" in a world where people increasingly "shop" for employment.

- Younger people make the distinction between talent and labor and increasingly are adopting the talent mind-set.

### Summary of Key Ideas

- The four working generations include matures, born from the beginning of the 20th century through 1945; baby boomers, born between 1946 and 1964; Generation X, born between

1965 and 1978; and Generation Y, born from 1979 to the late 1990s. Understanding the dynamics and interrelationships of these generations helps employers understand how their workers interact on the job.

- Older workers experienced the hierarchies of the manufacturing era, while younger workers view "Dilbert" as their metaphor to mock their feelings about bureaucratic work environments.

- Although many matures worked for the same company during most of their career, Gen Xers and Gen Yers will frequently change jobs *and* careers during their working life.

- Developing a strong employeecentric brand goes a long way toward establishing your reputation as an "employer of choice."

- As new generations enter the workforce, their values infiltrate and influence the other generations on the job.

- Younger workers are more likely to expect teamwork and collaboration on the job rather than authoritarianism.

- Family and lifestyle values are increasingly important for Gen Xers and Gen Yers, who also expect to receive lifestyle perks that support these values.

- Younger workers tend to embrace diversity issues more openly than matures or baby boomers.

- Older boomers will work longer and are reinventing retirement as we knew it.

- Demographic shifts in the workplace can be managed by keeping older workers on the job either as consultants or part-time workers.

- Mentoring opportunities exist that can bring together matures and older boomers with Gen Xers and Gen Yers as a way to bridge the experience gap.

## Thinking Points

- Review your workforce to analyze its generational composition.

- Based on your analysis, identify where your firm has potential employment weaknesses in the next five to ten years.

- Outline one idea that will position your firm to maximize its generational diversity.

- Host a brown-bag lunch where people can informally discuss generational values with each other.

- Identify ways that your firm can better utilize an aging workforce and an inexperienced, young workforce.

## CHAPTER 3

# Who Are Your People Anyway?

A perplexing aspect of today's world of work is that you don't know whether the people who work for you are actually your employees. They can be salaried employees or independent contractors. They may work full-time or part-time. They may work in the office or at home or on the road. The lines have blurred considerably, and it's not so easy to distinguish who is who. Furthermore, companies are able to tap into the personal network of contacts of key employees. These personal networks are becoming an increasingly important component of an individual's human asset value.

In the manufacturing-era model, who your people were was completely clear. Virtually all of the people who worked for a company were full-time workers accounted for on the payroll. They were W-2 employees who started their affiliation with you by filling out an application for employment. They interviewed for the job and sometimes took skills-based tests to prove their proficiency. After they were offered the job, they filled out the appropriate employment forms. They worked on your company premises for a regularly scheduled set of hours. They received a weekly or biweekly paycheck, benefits based on eligibility, and regular performance reviews. At the end of the year, you would submit a W-2 statement to the IRS that reflected how much they earned over the course of the year, and a new cycle would begin.

Today, full-time W-2 employees who work on-site are just one of many categories of people who work for your organization. Several different employment options exist. In fact, the salaried employee is a somewhat endangered species because the world of employment has changed dramatically. If you walk into a company meeting today, you probably don't know who is an employee and who is a consultant. The work of independent contractors is often the same work as that of salaried employees.

## Defining the Categories

### W-2 or Salaried Employees

These are traditional employees. You pay them wages, salaries, and benefits; and record this activity through your payroll tax contributions and IRS filings each year. On reaching eligibility, these employees can participate in the firm's pension or retirement plan. If the company offers a 401(k) plan, these employees can participate and are often eligible for a matching gift as an incentive to participate. Salaried employees tend to receive compensation that the company offers them. Although there may be some room for negotiation, the salary range is often fixed within a grade level. Only a relatively small group of progressive companies utilize pay-for-performance models that extend incentive compensation beyond executive and managerial levels. These companies understand that this is a way to retain workers who view themselves as talent that contributes to their employer's bottom line.

### Free Agents

Also known as independent contractors, these are workers who market freelance services to companies. Sometimes they do the same work as salaried staff, but the biggest distinction between them is that the freelance workers receive no benefits from the company. They are responsible for paying their own taxes and do not participate in any profit sharing, stock options, or other general benefits offered by the firm. Some independent contractors formerly worked for a company and were laid off or opted for early retirement and now work for the same firm without benefits.

Other free agents are people who don't want to be tied down to a traditional corporate lifestyle, so they work on their own. Most of these people see themselves as what they are—talent—and market themselves accordingly. They may work by themselves or run small businesses that rent their services to others.

### How salaried employees and free agents operate.

These two types of workers can operate under a number of different scenarios. They can work full-time in a normal workweek or on their own schedule. They can work part-time on their own schedule. They can work at the office. They can telecommute from home or a remote location. They can work from the road. They can work on-site with clients. They can be primary contractors or subcontractors. They can be tested or assessed and interviewed on multiple levels before being offered a position. They can be hired on a handshake through a referral.

Notice how many variations emerge from these different combinations. The mechanics of hiring and tracking workers takes on an entirely different, staggering complexity when you start imagining all of the different scenarios. Yet many companies operate with systems that support and track salaried employees only, when an increasingly larger proportion of their people are hired in nontraditional categories that didn't exist 20 or 40 years ago.

A fundamental change in the way people work for organizations, therefore, is that they work on their own terms, not the terms dictated by employers. The Ernst & Young Center for Business Innovations predicts that by the year 2010 less than half of the work done in U.S. companies will be done by full-time employees.[1] Although power has shifted from employers to workers, many employers are still operating within the outdated paradigm of the manufacturing era. Remember the distinction between talent and labor. Talent negotiates terms with an employer. Labor gets hired for the salary offered it.

## Temporary Workers

Another interesting outcome of the change in work structure and transiency is the increasing number of temporary (temp) workers, who appear in both traditional and new economy companies. Employment agencies place temp workers and provide them with traditional benefits based on the amount of time they work. Many temps are marking time until they get another permanent job, while others use temp jobs to evaluate companies they may want to work for. Others work in temp positions so they can pursue a creative career, such as acting or music.

The temp agency business has become more broad-based as workers can register on a short-term or long-term basis. Some 3.3 million workers are on temp ledgers. Manpower, Inc., in fact, claims to be the largest employer in the United States.[2] Hiring temps is a very good deal for some employers: The temp agency performs screening and testing; it takes care of benefits; and it takes back temps when companies no longer need them, avoiding the unpleasantness of firing.

A growing category is permanent temps, who often work full-time for a company but are not salaried. Some are placed by agencies, while others are independent contractors. Companies often hire permanent temps to manage their internal employee headcount as well as to avoid paying benefits. Permanent temp status can backfire and spawn bad feelings on the part of the temps, who may feel that the companies they work for take advantage of their temp status. The status is analogous to that of unmarried couples living together; although temp workers may not be married to the company, they are living together and are entitled to the same benefits permanent staffers receive. Employing temporary workers will always be popular, though, because it costs about 40 percent less to have them on the payroll than to have permanent workers.[3]

Companies have the ability to hedge their bets when it comes to hiring workers in different categories. Temporary workers or independent contractors can reduce the "official" headcount as well as represent a less costly alternative because they aren't receiving benefits. Decision makers need to weigh the benefits of a cheaper workforce against potentially less loyal independent contractors. Companies that contract nonsalaried workers who play an important and strategic role need to ensure that they make these workers feel valued. If they don't feel valued, they will leave.

## Free Agency: The Talent Model for the 21st Century

Free agents, as previously noted, are independent contractors who market freelance services to companies. Free agency was one of the most significant concepts to impact the employment world in the late 20th century. It is estimated that one of six workers is currently a free agent, and this number is projected to increase substantially over the next ten years. Although the expression *free agent* came into use during the rise of new economy companies, free agents are found in all industries. Daniel Pink, author of *Free Agent Nation* and an authority on the topic, believes that people become free agents as a way to lead a more satisfying life.[4] His theme diffuses the myth that free agents are grabbing for money and looking for the next dot-com get-rich-quick scheme.

## $W$ORKPLACE TREND

*Free agency is the model for employment in the 21st century.*

## The Value of Talent

In the old world of work, you were paid a salary that might increase a bit each year, based largely on longevity and seniority. But now, Pink comments, the pay-for-performance ethic is widespread whether people are compensated by stock options or by commissions. Free agents find that their market price fluctuates in much the same way that stock prices fluctuate. So it becomes much harder to establish the exact value of an individual from a corporate perspective. Pink suggests an analogy to a company's investment portfolio, in which today's value differs from tomorrow's; absent is a static fixed price that endures over time.

In *Blur: The Speed of Change in the Connected Economy,* Stan Davis and Christopher Meyer comment on economic implications for free agents.[5] They believe that everyone is a free agent and that frequent job changes are a testament to how the marketplace values talent. They predict that securitization of individuals is the next evolution, as already evidenced by Bowie bonds. These are bonds securitized by the future stream of revenue from royalties generated by musician David Bowie's recorded music and concerts. Although this trend is beginning with celebrities, it will eventually filter down to unknown free agents. Davis and Meyer make the point that people will raise money through the capital markets to achieve their goals the way companies have been doing for years.

Extrapolating from this, we could see a growing demand for a securities market in human capital. People would attach the equivalent of a 52-week trading range to themselves, which would fluctuate based on the work they have performed, and be paid according to the market supply and demand for their talent. Talent workers will accumulate experiences in their work "portfolio" that enhance the value of that portfolio. Free agents will work for your firm if they think the work they do will add to the value of their portfolio.

**❝** *Free agents will work for your firm if they think the work they do will add to the value of their portfolio.* **❞**

According to Pink:

Free agents can then price themselves based on what the market will bear. When free agents are evaluating projects, they are not basing them solely on money. They want to know that they are going to be working with good people, that they are working on projects that are interesting. They want something that will add to their portfolio of experience and talent. Perhaps they will have an opportunity to learn some new skills. Essentially, the financial price is part of a much larger calculation. Pricing then shifts, depending on what kind of value they are receiving in the other realms.

## Free Agency as an Employment Model

The free agent model is ready to become the employment model for the first part of the 21st century. The "war for talent" will persist regardless of the economy. There may be hundreds of thousands of people laid off, but talent will rise to the surface. Firms must hire talent to stay competitive.

People with hiring responsibility must be prepared for what a true free agent, unlike a traditional independent contractor, looks for in terms of working experience. The old model is one of an independent contractor taking work because it's work (the labor mentality), but a free agent takes work for the sake of growth. Pink believes organizations that accommodate and nurture talent are the ones that will survive—market efficiency will prevail. Companies that balk at the idea of hiring free agents or don't believe in paying a market price for talent will lose.

Increasingly, talent will be hired based on fluctuating market prices rather than on fixed salary ranges. In fact, it is possible to envision a time when an auction model will apply to talent. Imagine an eBay for talent where companies competitively bid for the people they want to hire. Forward-thinking companies realize that talent will increasingly demand a market price and that this price will fluctuate based on supply and demand. This is one of the key reasons why executives can begin to view talent as an investment and not a cost. A fixed salary range—regardless of performance—implies cost. Market pricing implies investment.

**❝** *It is easier to perceive talent as an investment when it is priced based on market supply and demand.* **❞**

## Global Workforce Transiency

The increased transiency of the workforce is a significant trend affecting the reorganization of work. People now work for smaller firms and don't work for the same companies for extended numbers of years. Worker mobility is prevalent. It is no longer a stigma to change jobs after a short period. On the contrary, in some industries, switching jobs regularly is seen as a badge of honor in contrast to the manufacturing-era model of people working as salaried employees for one company for their entire working life.

*W*ORKPLACE TREND

*The increasing transiency of the global workforce affects recruiting and hiring decisions, and talent will migrate to companies that value their people.*

One of the reasons why the workforce has become more transient has to do with our burgeoning 24/7 economy. In 1997, only 29.1 percent of employed workers worked a standard 35-to-40-hour workweek. Only 54.4 percent regularly worked a fixed daytime schedule during all five work days. Part-timers are more likely than full-timers to work for periods other than fixed days. A substantial demand exists for late-hour and weekend work that is spawned by the growth of the service sector and the 24/7 economy.[6]

**Telecommuting.** This has contributed to the increasing transiency in the workforce. It has become increasingly popular, although, depending on the economy, its prevalence fluctuates. Some 24 million employees telecommute regularly, which can offer tremendous savings to employers. Reduced absenteeism, increased productivity, and lower recruiting costs are some of the top reasons employers realize savings. On the other hand, a number of companies reject the idea of telecommuting. They feel that home-based workers build resentment among office-based workers because corporate loyalty is diminished. They also feel that telecommuters miss the informal gatherings of people in the office.[7] These firms feel that by not experiencing the collegial interaction, telecommuters may be less committed.

Companies that resist telecommuting miss the point. If office-based workers feel resentment, it's probably because they don't like the office environment. Concerns about decreased loyalty are unwarranted for two reasons. First, the concept of corporate loyalty isn't based on being tied to a desk at the main office. Second, some office-based workers think that telecommuters sit around all day and watch TV. On the contrary, home-based workers of all types tend to get more done in any eight-hour period than they would in the office.

We think of telecommuters as home-based or remote-based workers in the field. Fewer in number, but potentially growing, is a subcategory of "extreme telecommuters." These are full-time salaried workers whose goal is to "happily blur the line between working and having an adventure,"[8] and thus allowing virtual workers to be employed while they travel around the world. People who work for companies that support telecommuting have a world of opportunity available to combine work and personal travel. Don't expect everyone to move to Bali and work on the beach, but this small trend is likely to increase, particularly among younger workers who haven't yet invested a lot of time in an office.

**Outsourcing.** Outsourcing is a trend that gathered momentum in the 1990s, becoming popular particularly as a way for manufacturers to manage their direct capital investment. These companies discovered that it is often better to outsource activities that are outside their core competencies. The growth of outsourcing is directly related to the increasing importance of human capital. Companies that outsource well are growing their people in their strongest area of competency. They pick outsource partners based on the way they manage and develop their intellectual and human capital.

**They work *where?*** For years, manufacturing companies have outsourced work to different parts of the world where their products can be produced more cheaply. An increasing amount of work for service businesses is being done overseas as well. The motivation for overseas work for service businesses is somewhat different, however, as it is often triggered by labor shortages in the United States. One interesting example is the call-center business that has seen a tremendous increase in demand for customer service representatives but a dearth of available operators. The solution? Establish call centers overseas.

Today you can call the customer service line of your favorite catalogue, and the call may be routed to a person in India or Ireland or the Philippines. Companies are training these outsourced workers to have midwestern accents, so you'd never know the difference. You may think that you are talking to somebody in Wisconsin when the person is actually in Bangalore. This will happen more frequently, especially as the cost of long-distance service, sophistication of telecommunications equipment, and the readily available and trainable workers abroad support this activity.

**Geographic mobility of labor and talent.** People will migrate around the country for work when motivated by an economic incentive. Such a movement occurred when the viability of the industrial Northeast faded and the manufacturing era began to decline. The established, industrial towns of the Northeast underwent significant deterioration as many workers from those communities migrated to the Southeast and Southwest looking for new opportunities. In this case, workers moved away from economic hardship in search of a better life. This has been the trend for labor—to move away in reaction to a declining employment proposition, not knowing whether the move will result in a better situation.

Contrast this with a contemporary migration story, the high-tech migration, which originated in Silicon Valley and was replicated in places like Route 128 in Boston, the Virginia suburbs of Washington, D.C., and Austin, Texas. Talent migrates to communities that are starving for human capital; it moves toward opportunity. Talent migrates to where it can work with other talent to create innovative products and services.

66 *Talent migrates to communities that are starving for human capital; it moves toward opportunity.* 99

Quality of life is another factor that can stimulate migration to a new geographic area. In recent decades, we have seen knowledge workers leave everything behind in their successful, urban worlds and move to the country or the mountains or the seashore to capture a more nourishing way of living. To be sure, technology makes this even more possible. If you have a telephone line and a modem, you can work almost anywhere. Soon you won't even need the phone line, as wireless and satellite technology become more reliable and cost-effective.

Talent gravitates to other talent. It's unlikely that we'll find lots of free agents living on a mountaintop. They may go there to decompress, but they want to be in communities of like-minded people where they work. Some experts feel that free agents identify with where they live because they aren't tied to a corporate identity. Cities are important, then, as places where free agents congregate. Free agents are attracted to urban-oriented amenities, fun, tolerance, and a place to which they can tie their identity.[9]

**Immigration shifts.** The United States has been an employment magnet for immigrants from countries around the world. Historically, people have emigrated here to overcome political or religious oppression or lack of economic opportunity in their native countries. A number of these immigrants lack education and skill and thus have taken lower-level jobs. Others have become entrepreneurs and business owners. In New York City, for example, the green grocers across the city are owned and operated primarily by Korean immigrants.

Immigrants now make up 12 percent of the American labor force, the highest level since the immigration wave of the early 20th century. Although labor unions are arguing against increasing immigrant quotas, they are softening their stance on illegal immigrants. Even the AFL-CIO has called for the repeal of a law barring employers from hiring illegal immigrants. Currently, it is estimated that 5 million illegal immigrants live in the United States.[10] They perform manual labor and work in jobs that the poorest Americans won't touch. Many economists believe that this population contributes significantly to American prosperity.

In recent years, however, a subtle shift in migration trends has been noted. A significant number of educated immigrants have come to the United States to achieve new levels of professional experience. Whereas some have made this their permanent home, others have worked in American companies and then taken the experience and expertise back to companies in their native countries. The high-tech industry is a good example of this. Significant numbers of high-tech workers, particularly from India and other East Asian countries, moved here to get exposure and broaden their horizons.

These highly educated, professional-level immigrants represent yet another category of workers in corporate America, adding more texture to the employment mosaic. Companies are willing to sponsor these workers under the H1-B visa program because they are highly educated technology workers who fill the much-needed gap in the booming information technology companies. Expect the global migration of these workers to increase. Information technology (IT) engineers are being recruited from India to Japan, Singapore, Germany, Ireland, and the UK. The United States gets half of its IT quota from India.[11]

This has been good news and bad news. The H1-B visa program requires workers to be employed in order to continue immigrant eligibility. During an economic downturn, such as the one the technology industry experienced in 2000 through 2001, new human capital challenges arose for employers. As these employers laid off massive numbers of people during this period, the status of H1-B workers became uncertain. They were not able to remain in the country if they weren't working, but they didn't want to leave precipitously if there was the possibility of being hired back. Because they need company sponsorship to continue residing in the United States, they can remain here only if another company hires them.

**International migration.** Worker mobility is much more prevalent in the United States than in Europe and Asia.[12] That said, it is becoming increasingly commonplace in Europe for people to take jobs in other countries. Some countries are blessed with high levels of employment and increasing demand for workers. Others suffer from high rates of unemployment. In some industries the supply and demand of jobs is leveling. This trend is more prevalent, however, among younger people, who see foreign opportunities as a way to enhance their experience and ultimately their human asset value.

One of the issues that we face as a global society in the coming years is chronic worker shortages in many countries in the developed world. Simply put, the number of older people is outpacing the number of births, already an issue in major countries in Europe, China, and Japan. At the present rate, these countries will not be able to keep businesses and social services running without looking abroad for qualified workers. To put this problem in context, Europe will be required to add some 35 million additional people by 2020 to keep its population at 1995 levels.[13] Japan faces a similar challenge; it needs to add 600,000 additional people per year for the next 50 years to maintain its 1995 population.

Again we face the issue of talent versus labor. Talent migrates to companies—wherever they are—that foster and cultivate human assets.

### *W*ORKPLACE TREND

*Talent migrates globally to companies that foster and cultivate human assets.*

## Working around the Clock

Increasingly, firms require people to work on a 24/7 basis. Roughly 40 percent of employed Americans work mostly evenings, weekends, or rotating shifts,[14] a situation largely evolving from the service sector—from retail fulfillment to home health care. We can expect that nontraditional work time, primarily nights and weekends, will increase as a result of 24/7. Much of the demand is for lower-level employees to service the 24/7 economy; and it is primarily women and minorities who will fill the jobs.

Our circadian rhythms are affected by operating in 24/7 time. Disruption results in a range of maladies from sleep disturbances to intestinal disorders to overall malaise and depression. Supplements such as melatonin are increasingly in demand, as they offset the disoriented feeling that people get from biophysical disorders. Social relationships, particularly those with family and friends, can be severely disrupted. Parents often work on opposite shifts so that each parent has some daily time with their children.

As a consequence, people feel increasingly out of sync. Working the all-night shift or traveling frequently makes them feel physically disoriented. Too much work and too little leisure causes them to feel out of balance with their life. In some firms, people work such incredibly long hours that incidences of "desk rage" have been reported. In a study of workplace stress, 42 percent of office workers said they work in places where shouting and verbal abuse occur frequently.[15]

Demand for around-the-clock workers creates new challenges for companies. Firms that require employees to work nontraditional schedules must come up with ways to sustain those workers. Firms that go the extra mile by providing support services will be perceived as benevolent places to work. For example, childcare arrangements can be made for women who work overnight as data entry operators. Another possibility is to rotate people through regular shifts so that no one group of workers is disadvantaged.

## The Network Multiplier

Networking became a popular and important activity for professionals in the 1990s. It has become particularly important for free agents as a method to expand their group of contacts. It has evolved to the stage where a person's personal network can be so extensive that it is a component of his or her human capital value. Having a large network of contacts while working in sales and marketing, for example, is a tremendous added value. Employers tend to hire people for their competency but also to tap into their networks, which further muddles the question of who your people are because an employer doesn't know the people in someone's network.

Cultivating workers' personal networks, then, is a key value-creating activity that companies can foster. Firms that encourage and support this activity will benefit. Networking results in contacts, referrals, introductions, and leads and is the starting point for building long-term relationships. Most important, the network becomes an extension of the person, meaning that the collective networks of *your people* are de facto additions to the value of your firm.

*O*NE SIZE DOESN'T FIT ALL

### Valuing Your Network

As a worker, your network is increasingly becoming an important part of your value as a human asset. Companies are interested in workers who know a wide range of people, particularly if the workers are in revenue-generating positions. Everyone's network is different, and the value of networks differs depending on how well people "work" them. People who actively stay in touch with members of their network receive much more value from their network than people who simply retain names in a database. People who stay connected with their network will be rewarded for who they know.

## Networks as Connectors

Warren Bennis observes that by their very nature, networks connect people to each other, which differs from the traditional corporate hierarchy, where people are basically told with whom they can communicate.[16] The emergence of networks, then, is a natural consequence of the development of talent and human capital. Increasingly, you will find the extent and scope of an individual's network to be a significant factor in hiring. People who have substantial numbers of contacts bring a wider opportunity of value to their organizations.

Harvey Mackay, president of a Minneapolis-based envelope company, is better known as a motivational speaker, author, and expert on networking. He is a master networker, who does his homework before meeting someone and learns seemingly amazing information before the meeting. The information is not really amazing. What is amazing is that he takes the time to do a bit of research. On meeting the person, Mackay uses a tidbit of information as a point of connection, and he receives instant credibility. In his book *Swim With the Sharks Without Being Eaten Alive,* Mackay puts his method to paper in the "Mackay 66," a list that originated as a template for his salespeople to use in developing relationships with clients.[17]

## Specialized Networks

Your professional women benefit by networking with their peers. Often excluded from the old boy network, women need to proactively cultivate their own contacts in order to expand their professional reach. Most prosperous people embrace their networks as leverage to help them achieve success. They form networks within their company and externally. It is important, however, that your female employees not restrict their network only to other women, which can be a stifling limitation. Women who work in traditionally male-oriented industries, in particular, need to develop a robust network. Sometimes it can make the difference between getting ahead or being pushed into a corner.

85 Broads is a women's networking organization formed by women who formerly worked for Goldman Sachs.[18] Catherine Banat, a Wall Street veteran and founding member of 85 Broads, now runs C3

Capital, a business built around connecting people and capital from her networks. Banat observed that in order to succeed, women needed to support each other in the elite ranks of financial institutions.[19] Many women operated in isolation as the only woman in a department. The women who worked at Goldman shared a credential that bred confidence. Connecting after they left was easy because of the shared culture and "breeding" that came from the Goldman experience.

Banat believes it is necessary to tap multiple networks and that the collective value of these networks adds to people's value as free agents. In addition to traditional venues, such as alumni groups, professional organizations, and affinity groups, she stresses the importance of informal networks. Banat recommends that your people cultivate informal networks in your business and across your firm as well as in your firm and across other businesses. For example, a money market professional at Goldman Sachs may have an informal network of people in the money market industry as well as a network throughout Goldman in equities, asset management, and other areas. A person's associate class creates the foundation to build a network.

It is also important for your people to broaden their horizons beyond your industry. Encourage them to create a dialogue with people in other industries, such as a financial services professional connecting with people who work in the telecommunications industry or brand management. Banat emphasizes that people tend to receive more value by networking with a group than from meeting one-on-one. The group dynamic generates more junctures for exchange. The importance of nurturing your network is even more important when you're a free agent, Banat says. She agrees that a person's network is a large part of his or her value as a human asset. "We are *who* we know and *what* we know. *What* I know is what allows me to know *who* to call."

**Networking Your Board of Directors.** Your board of directors or board of advisors is another network of resources. Board members can cultivate relationships and provide introductions and leads to their firms. Companies value directors who bring in strategic relationships. As companies build their boards, they should keep in mind that directors who add value through their networks have the potential to create a different level of relationship capital. Outside of its relationship with the company, it is important that the director be an advocate for the company. CEOs who use their board members as truly trusted advisors are able to leverage that person's human capital and network.[20]

**Alumni networks.** Alumni groups are a great networking resource for your people. Academic alumni associations are important links for reconnecting with people as well as making contacts specifically for business. When someone makes a cold call to a person from his alma mater, he will probably get in the door. Some successful free agents look up alumni when they travel on business. They make contact with one or two people just to connect and expand their reach. These relationships are often untapped, and it can be extremely worthwhile for you to encourage your people to nurture them.

Chapter 5 explores the increasing phenomenon of corporate alumni networks, whose purpose is to provide a way for current and former employees to stay connected with each other. These networks have been successful in the consulting and financial services industries, in particular, where alumni of your organization could become your clients tomorrow.

## Final Thoughts

This chapter began by distinguishing between salaried employees and free agents. Without question, the boundaries are blurring; today, it isn't visibly apparent who is a free agent and who is a salaried employee. Eventually, it will be irrelevant. Successful companies will seek talent; having the right talent for the right task is what matters. Companies must cast aside the hierarchical corporate mind-set and think about where they can capture the talent. The perfect person for that new project may be as close as around the globe. Hiring the best people for the job and treating them as valued workers will make a difference in your company's productivity and profitability.

An important human capital strategy is to develop lifetime affiliation with anyone associated with your firm, whether a salaried employee, free agent, temp, outsourcing partner, foreign worker, or board member. Because everyone who comes into contact with your company gets an impression, you want a positive image to be reflected in the market. This can be achieved by building solid relationships with the people associated with your firm, regardless of the length of time they have worked with you. Everyone then becomes a part of your network, and the relationship continues.

**66** *Relationships are the building blocks of human capital.* **99**

Relationships are the building blocks of human capital and are important at all levels. It doesn't matter whether the person draws a salary or receives a lump sum for a project. It's all the same in the end, and the blurring will continue. Invest in relationships with your people, and you'll receive dividends for years to come.

## CHAPTER RECAP

### Workplace Trends

- Free agency is the model for employment in the 21st century.

- The increasing transiency of the global workforce affects recruiting and hiring decisions, and talent will migrate to companies that value their people.

- Talent migrates globally to companies that foster and cultivate human assets.

### Summary of Key Ideas

- The two basic categories of workers—salaried employees and free agents—work in any number of ways: full-time, part-time, in the office, telecommuting from home, working from the road, 9 to 5, midnight to 8, temporary, or permanent. The boundaries between salaried employees and free agents are blurring.

- Free agents view themselves as talent and choose the work that will add value to their portfolio of experiences.

- As people "securitize" their future earnings, a capital market for talent may emerge.

- People migrate to jobs where their talent can be best used.

- Some 24 million people telecommute regularly, a form of work likely to continue.

- Outsourcing is a way that companies can concentrate their human capital on their firm's core competencies.

- Educated workers from around the world will migrate to countries that can use their talent.

- Global migration will increase well into the 21st century based on significant needs for replacement immigration in countries where the birth rate isn't keeping pace with the aging population.

- Companies' 24/7 work time schedules affect workers physically, with their circadian rhythms causing biophysical and social disorientation. Companies need to address this issue if they manage a 24/7 workforce.

- Employers attach value to a person's network. When they hire a highly connected person, they receive the benefit of that person's network.

- Lifetime affiliation with your people creates long-term relationships for your company.

## Thinking Points

- Identify who your people are. Evaluate the pros and cons of your staff as currently configured.

- Meet with key colleagues and determine which strategies you will implement to support your desired workforce. For example, your firm may have resisted a telecommuting strategy but now sees value in creating a telecommuting pilot program.

- Evaluate the functions that your firm outsources. Are you maximizing these opportunities so you can build on your firm's core competencies?

- Facilitate your people's ability to network across your organization. Proactively encourage networking in professional associations and affinity groups.

- Think about how you can create lifetime affiliations with your people so your firm benefits from these relationships in the long run.

# PART TWO

# Measuring Human Capital

*This part explores aspects of measuring human capital. Because many of these aspects are cutting-edge, they are not included in financial reporting under generally accepted accounting principles. Companies can undertake this kind of quantification and analyze results for improved operations. Some firms take it a step further by voluntarily disclosing nonfinancial measurements as a supplement to their financial reporting. In either case, companies that take the time to capture, record, and track such information will enhance their results because they have a much better opportunity to understand the productivity of their human capital.*

## CHAPTER 4

# Valuing Human Capital

Attempting to attach measurements to people is a daunting challenge. After all, people are living organisms that change. Is your personal value different today than it was yesterday? Did your value change as a result of working on a new and innovative project at work? Or did it change because you volunteered at your local community center last weekend and were profoundly moved by a conversation with a homeless person? Does your value go down when you have the flu or go up after you've run a marathon? Does a person with a Ph.D. have a higher value than one with a GED? Does the CEO have a higher value than the janitor?

This is provocative stuff. And your willingness to explore pioneering concepts, such as measuring human capital, corroborates the idea that we are at the forefront of a fundamental change in the way we value our businesses. The mere attempt to measure intangible assets creates a new benchmark. We are, in effect, challenging that our 500-year-old accounting system doesn't work for idea- and innovation-based companies that generate substantial revenue and profits from intangible capital.

To measure human capital, you need to evaluate nonfinancial data. Firms that want to assess the impact of their human capital practices need to capture, track, and record data that will result in a body of information that can then be analyzed to determine linkages. Ultimately, the goal of such measurement, as with other intangibles, is to increase your company's return on investment.

Chapter 1 addressed the evolution of capital as a means of wealth creation. Capital was first valued from natural resources, such as land, evolving to capital derived from machines and factories. Then financial capital became the primary means of wealth generation. Now, it seems that we've come full circle back to natural resources. This time, though, *people are the natural resource*. We can look at this another way by observing changes in the role of property. Historically, we have been buyers and sellers of products, but ownership is being replaced by access. Jeremy Rifkin, author, futurist, and Fellow of the Wharton School Executive Education Program, tells us that suppliers of products "hold on to property in the New Economy, and lease, rent, or charge an admission fee, subscription or membership dues for its short-term use."[1] Wealth is now investment in human imagination and creativity, not in physical capital. The growing importance of human capital substantiates this point: Companies have the short-term use of a person's brain and creativity. By "renting" human capital, a firm can significantly expand its wealth-generating capacity.

This chapter introduces some of the cutting-edge research in the area of valuing human capital. The body of research is quite large, so examples are merely snapshots of current thinking by leading policy-makers and researchers. Brief research summaries convey the types of information that firms can capture, record, and track with the ultimate goal of creating meaningful measures in your firm. You can then consider ways to convert this theory and research into a foundation for measuring human capital in your company.

## Measuring Unmeasurables

The challenge in measuring intangibles such as human capital is that, by definition, intangibles are not measurable. The real challenge is to identify things that can be quantified and set up a pilot program to provide measures for things previously considered nonquantifiable.

### *W*ORKPLACE TREND

*Companies are creating ways to measure their return on intangible assets.*

Laurie J. Bassi, president of Human Capital Dynamics, has performed leading-edge research in measuring human capital. She was the chair of the Human Capital subgroup of the Brookings Institution task force on intangibles. Brookings brought together top researchers and practitioners to study the economic impact of intangibles in our society. Formerly vice president of research for the American Society of Training and Development (ASTD), Bassi spearheaded a massive survey designed to understand how companies measure the impact of training. One outcome of this research revealed a correlation between a company's stock performance and its investment in training.

Bassi observes that measuring human capital is a bigger issue for larger, bureaucratic companies than it is for smaller ones. "The industrial era mind-set, where all of the reasons why people can't make these things happen, are embedded in policy, rules, and procedures which are much more rigid in larger organizations than in smaller organizations." [2]

One of Bassi's discoveries was that many larger companies have no significant internal reporting procedures in place. For example, some of the companies that participated in her research studies have not had readily available information pertaining to training and education, which may seem surprising as these are data that can be quantified. Bassi acknowledges that intangibles are hard to measure. "Yet we must learn to measure. We must learn, if not direct measures, at least indirect measures. If [intangibles are] the source of wealth creation, we have to manage it. Which means we have to measure it. Which means we *have* to figure out how to do this, even though it's not easy."

It's clear that valuing intangibles is filled with incongruities. The accounting profession, for example, has been reluctant to take a strong position. Accountants know that valuing intangibles is an important topic, but they want to maintain audit integrity by addressing what is certain. They feel that intangibles are too elusive and soft to measure. After years of discussion, various policy and governing entities, ranging from the Financial Accounting Standards Board (FASB) to the American Institute of CPAs (AICPA) to the Securities and Exchange Commission (SEC), will not make concrete recommendations. On the other hand, virtually all of the consulting divisions of the top CPA firms are marketing products that give clients tools to measure intangibles. Each firm has a proprietary variation of a human capital measurement instrument, for example. Although accounting policy leaders have not taken a concrete stand on ways to measure intangibles, their consulting colleagues have felt free to commercialize products that measure them.

KPMG partner Robert K. Elliott has affirmed the importance of the accounting profession taking bold new tactics to disclose the value of intangibles. As a former chairman of the AICPA, Elliott has participated in policy discussions on accounting and disclosure for intangibles. He feels there is a framing problem, meaning that accountants confine the practice of accounting to financial information. "They haven't generalized the set of skills that they have as being people with talents, figuring out what needs to be measured, and measuring it for the benefit of decision makers."[3] The mistake is that accountants define themselves as being in the financial business rather than in the information business.

Elliott admits that the important aspects of knowledge assets, such as leadership, teamwork, and creativity, are very difficult to measure. He remarks, "Capital is fungible; it can be applied to disparate projects with good effect. Human resources are particular. A highly qualified physicist cannot be substituted for a highly skilled mason."[4]

Natural resources, capital resources, and technology resources are no longer the main constraints on economic development, Elliott states. Instead, the challenge is talent. "The way in which an economy develops talent and deploys that talent is going to be the main determinant of [its] success." He acknowledges that accountants develop, build, and maintain the infrastructure to help move capital to its highest investment: financial capital. "But nobody currently builds and develops the infrastructure to move talent to its highest investment. And that is a very different question when moving capital for two reasons. One is that capital is fungible and your dollar and my dollar can both be put to exactly the same use. Talent is not fungible because we have very different talents. The other reason is that financial capital is very passive, whereas human capital is very active."

Today, human capital drives business. And human capital has become *the* scarce resource. By measuring human capital, then, we have the potential to quantify how that capital is being used to create additional wealth. Companies compete for talent. Talent leases itself to firms often for an unknown period. Your firm will never own it, yet it is the source for value creation—another incongruity. When talented employees feel it is time to move on, they walk out of your building on Friday and don't return on Monday. At that point, you hope that enough other people on your team were familiar with their work so you can continue with relatively little disruption. Otherwise, you may have lost a lot of future value from the time lost in reconstructing work in process or cultivating client relationships anew.

**❝** *Human capital has become* the *scarce resource.* **❞**

New York University Professor Baruch Lev is a leading expert on intangibles, whose ideas have been featured in numerous articles in the business press.[5] As a participant in the Brookings task force on intangibles, Lev was asked to present his research ideas and recommend reforms for the accounting and disclosure of intangibles.[6]

Lev makes the distinction between reporting and disclosure of financial information. Human capital measurements fall under the category of disclosure, meaning that this information could be cited in the footnotes to a company's financial statements but not in the financial statements themselves. Lev recommends that companies record systematic information on key variables, such as training, incentive-based compensation, and turnover. "If you start disclosing these numbers, you are giving some very important tools to people to evaluate human resource practices."[7] After tracking several years of data on training, for example, Lev would like to look at some correlation between "increases in training expenses and perhaps decreases in turnover, and some measures of productivity which I can compute from the financial report like sales and employees. This will start giving me some analytical tools—not just pieces of information—real analytical tools to evaluate measurement."

Lev makes the important point that the information that companies voluntarily disclose to outsiders has a huge effect on what managers actually do internally. For example, if companies disclose data about their investment in training and development, they are more likely to proactively manage human capital. Even when companies use a balanced scorecard or similar measure internally, it's not what the CFO recalls at the top of his mind when meeting with analysts. "Whenever I talk about this, the CFO will say, 'It's interesting, but financial analysts don't ask this information from us.' Not yet. I'm sure they will, but whatever is disclosed has a huge effect inside. This means that if they don't disclose information on human resources, they most likely do not use it internally either."

If people don't record the data, they won't have anything to measure. "Unless you instruct someone to start recording these things," Lev comments, "you won't have this in the regular accounts." Tracking data leads to the ability to create linkages to outcomes.

Companies need to start by capturing and tracking these data. Once you have gathered a sufficient amount, you can begin to analyze it.

## Implications for Shareholder Value

Measuring human capital can have a payoff in the form of higher share price. There is a widening gap, previously noted, between a company's market value and book value, particularly in knowledge-based companies.[8] In 1998, book value was just 28 percent of market value.[9] Although this differential may narrow during times of economic downturn and depressed stock markets, there will still be a gap. While experts may differ on mathematical accounting for this gap, clearly it reflects the increasing level of intangibles. Service industries have grown steadily as a percent of gross domestic product (GDP), and intangibles comprise a substantial part of value in service companies. Over time, companies that create a system to capture, record, and measure data on human capital will be able to identify specific linkages between human capital strategies and share price. Remember that these are linkages, not absolutes. Look for patterns, not certainty.

66 *Measuring human capital can have a payoff in the form of higher share prices.* 99

Ineffective human capital decisions can have an adverse effect on shareholder value as well. A Bain and Company survey of 288 Fortune 500 companies revealed that stock prices of companies that dismissed more than 3 percent of their employees performed no better than those that made fewer or no cuts. Furthermore, share prices of companies that cut more than 15 percent of their workforce performed substantially below average.[10]

During the high-tech bubble, Microsoft surpassed General Electric (GE) as the company with the largest market capitalization. Then, for a short time, Cisco's market capitalization surpassed Microsoft's. Each of these companies had a high proportion of intangibles, but GE had proportionately more tangible assets. Microsoft's market value was a dazzling 24 times book value by the time its market capitalization exceeded $500 billion. This occurrence shattered all previous conceptions of the relationship between market and book values. Microsoft and Cisco were often cited as representative of "inflated and unrealistically valued" new economy companies. It was also the wake-up call, though, that alerted people to the growing importance of intangibles.

New economy companies' market capitalization returned to more realistic levels after the 2000–2001 stock market decline. In effect, the higher market capitalizations in the peak valuations of 1999 only made sense if you assumed that these companies could continue growing at historical rates of growth. That obviously wasn't going to happen. Nonetheless, intangibles continue to drive these new economy companies. To wit, think about Bill Gates's reliance on his "brain trust," an exclusive group of engineers—his inner circle—who are his influential advisors.[11] You may not be able to directly link this brain trust to share price, but the innovation and product development that emerges from this human capital clearly contributes significantly to Microsoft's market value.

CEOs need to share the information on linkages between intangibles—including human capital—and share price with their boards. It is important that your directors understand how underlying intellectual capital value contributes to shareholder value. By clearly understanding this connection, everyone is more committed to delivering value to your shareholders.[12] A good example is the California Public Employees' Retirement System (CalPERS), the largest public pension fund in the United States. Under the guidance of Bob Boldt, senior investment officer, CalPERS has used nontraditional methods to extract value from stocks. His methods influenced William Crist, head of the CalPERS board, to recommend modernizing the governance practices of the companies' boards of directors. The three strongest indicators of long-term value in the companies have become (1) the creation of independent boards of directors, (2) human capital development, and (3) pay for performance. Boldt says that the key is to "create pay plans that give employees incentives that generate both a sense of ownership and a feeling of leverage over the company's performance."[13]

## WORKPLACE TREND

*A company's intangible capital is an increasingly important contributor to shareholder value.*

## The Need for Standardization

Until a standard is established, companies will create independent measures to record and track their intangibles. Although commendable, it makes more sense to create some sort of standardization. Intangibles will expand in importance as more knowledge-based companies come into existence. If nothing else, standardization means that every company won't have to reinvent the wheel each time it wants to track a new piece of data.

### Activities of Policymakers

The SEC appointed a task force in April 2000 to identify ways companies can make more disclosures about intangibles. John Doerr, a task force member and partner in a Silicon Valley venture capital firm, recommends that the task force consider measurements of things like the lifetime value of a customer and the cost of acquiring new customers. Tracking the amount of revenue generated from new products in a given year, moreover, is a way to identify a firm's innovativeness.[14]

The Financial Accounting Standards Board (FASB) has been working on standardization as well. Its Business Reporting Research Project reveals what companies in a variety of different industries are doing in the area of voluntary reporting. The premise of its report is that "improving disclosures makes the capital allocation process more efficient and reduces the average cost of capital." Relatively little is mentioned in the area of reporting intangibles; what was agreed is that more information is needed about those intangible assets. As defined in this report, intangibles include human resources, customer relationships, and innovations.[15]

The Brookings study was motivated by a belief that intangible assets are increasing in economic importance and they exact costs on our society as long as we don't account for them. The study maintained that although traditional income statement accounting for labor makes sense, accounting measures do not reflect future benefits that come from training, teambuilding, and other organizational development activities. The Brookings study acknowledged the measurement challenges surrounding human capital. Although employees can take their knowledge and ideas with them when they leave, firms cannot force them to leave this intellectual capital behind. The study did conclude, however, that "a firm's personnel, management, and training policies may have a very large effect on the productivity, innovativeness, and profitability of a firm."[16]

Specifically, Baruch Lev recommends a comprehensive information standard. A standard scorecard "portraying the innovation process of businesses and focusing on the intangible investment-generating process will drive a larger number of companies to provide new and useful information, internally and externally."[17] He also recommends "a considerable broadening of the current rules of asset recognition to include technologically feasible intangibles with attributable benefits."

## Management Tools

Nonpolicymakers have created management tools that address disclosing information about intangibles, a number of which are already in practice. The "balanced scorecard," created by Robert Kaplan and David Norton in 1992, was one of the first methodologies to select and measure nonfinancial performance indicators. The Malcolm Baldridge Award for Quality is a nonfinancial methodology that became popular in the 1990s. Total Quality Management (TQM) was another methodology; and Customer Relationship Management (CRM) evolved specifically as a way to measure customer-related performance.

John Bourdeau, director of Cornell University's Center for Advanced Human Resource Studies, and Pete Ramstad of Personnel Decisions International created the Human Capital Bridge, which links what people do with the value they create in a company. They look for the relation between human capital metrics and an organization's goals. Linkages take into account such things as organizational strategy changes, focus on a firm's core competencies, and the ability to quantify and analyze outcomes of human capital data tracking.[18]

Global services firm Skandia has been a pioneer in measuring and voluntarily disclosing information about intangibles to their shareholders. The company divides its market value into two components: financial capital and intellectual capital. Financial capital is essentially composed of the reported information in the annual report, while intellectual capital represents the "hidden values" of the company. Intellectual capital is divided into customer capital, organizational capital, and human capital. For information sharing and knowledge tracking, Skandia employees proactively use an intranet, which records the essence of the structural capital, or what is left behind after people leave the office.

The Skandia Navigator is a future-oriented business-planning model that provides a balanced overall picture of the company's operations. It balances the past (the financial focus), the present (customer, human, and process focus), and the future (renewal and development focus).[19] The Navigator links the company's vision and values to employees' individual work. Skandia's intranet enables managers to track data and compare their experience to other Skandia companies. Managers can access the intranet to look at best practices in other countries. They can then assess whether there are good ideas that can be applied locally. The corporate culture of Skandia rewards use of this knowledge-sharing tool so people are willing to share information.

Skandia is one of the first companies to have published a supplement to its annual report to shareholders, in which it disclosed information on intellectual capital. Its 1998 supplement featured extensive information about human capital, which was divided into three components: competence, relationships, and values. The supplement also attempted to quantify the impact of human capital by showing its base value, relationship value, and potential value. Skandia utilizes ratios provided by the Key Ratio Institute in Stockholm, an enterprise that is creating various human capital indicators.[20]

## Research Studies

A wealth of research has emerged in recent years related to measuring intangibles in general and human capital specifically. Although there is no one "definitive" study, the diverse research is converging to support the opinion that capturing, tracking, and recording data will result in a body of information that can then be analyzed to determine linkages between human capital strategies and profitability. Ultimately, the goal of such measurements is to increase return on investment. More specifically, though, you want to see which investments in human capital development will result in proportionately increased productivity and profitability.

The following are highlights from a sampling of the studies. Please keep in mind that there are many studies on this topic.

The American Society of Training and Development (ASTD). ASTD set up a benchmarking system for companies on discovering that companies had no idea how much they were spending on training and education, let alone what kind of return they were getting. Laurie Bassi was vice president of research for ASTD at the time. The organization essentially broke down all of the component expenses related to training and education, and requested specific information from the companies. At the beginning of the research, it was clear that many of the companies did not even capture the data that is necessary to evaluate returns on training.

By mid-2000, ASTD had collected information from more than 2,500 firms covering training-related expenditures. Of those firms, 575 were publicly traded, allowing ASTD to link its research data to the companies' public financial information. ASTD looked at how investments in training affected total shareholder return (TSR) the following year. It found that "firms that spend more than average on training have TSRs that are 86 percent higher than firms that spend less than average, and 45 percent higher than the market average."[21]

Conclusions from ASTD's research indicate that businesses improve their market valuation when they invest in training and that investors could improve their portfolio performance if they had access to that information. Bassi observes that human resources professionals whose companies participated in the study are now able to have serious conversations with their CEOs and CFOs. "They've got something to talk about—how they compare, where they stack up, where they see their strengths and weaknesses, and what it would mean for the organization to do things differently."

Human Capital Dynamics. Bassi is continuing her research into the correlation between training and total shareholder return. The current research offers an investment proposition: If companies that invest relatively high amounts in training create above-average total shareholder returns, why not consider the stock of these companies an investment opportunity?[22] Bassi, in fact, recently formed an investment management company, Knowledge Asset Management, that will do just that—invest in firms that have relatively high investments in training.

The Gallup Organization. Gallup is a world leader in the measurement and analysis of human attitudes, opinions, and behavior. It has interviewed more than a million employees since the mid-1970s on every imaginable aspect of the workplace. Two of its consultants, Marcus Buckingham and Curt Coffman, seized the opportunity to sort through Gallup's gigantic amount of information to look for the key elements of workplace strength. They discovered that it could be simplified to 12 questions that capture the greatest amount of, and the most important, information. In substantiating their research, they found that the most important indicator of an employee's success was his or her immediate manager. If managers treat people well and bring out their best, the employees are likely to be engaged and productive. Buckingham and Coffman's methodology and commentary are contained in *First, Break All the Rules.*[23]

The questions the authors raise point to measures of productivity, customer satisfaction, profitability, and retention—all of which can be captured, recorded, and tracked. Their analysis focuses on having the right people placed in the right jobs, having an opportunity to do your best and be recognized for it, and having sufficient resources to do your job well. Managers who follow these guidelines will enhance their ability to attract, retain, and motivate their people.

**Cap Gemini Ernst & Young's Center for Business Innovation (CBI).** CBI has conducted a number of studies of human capital. *Twenty Questions about Knowledge Management* revealed that focused internal management of knowledge leads to greater firm benefits that include improved innovation, increased flexibility, and increased responsiveness to customers. Managers expressed an interest in measuring data such as revenue generated by new ideas, but many feel that their corporate culture prevents such measuring. Even though managers see the value in knowledge management, it is curious that few were really interested in the contributions employees were actually making to the organization's bank of knowledge.[24]

Another CBI project, the *Capital Markets Study,* amassed information from portfolio managers and traders. The survey presented scenarios requiring participants to allocate their investment dollars among the companies presented in the scenarios. Some of the questions in the survey focused on nonfinancial information, including human capital measures. Analysis revealed that 35 percent of the portfolio allocation decisions were based on the nonfinancial information. The researchers concluded that factors such as a firm's management experience, its people's skills, and its people's alignment with company goals were leading indicators of performance.[25]

CBI partnered with the Wharton School at the University of Pennsylvania and *Forbes ASAP* to conduct an Internet survey for determining the extent to which companies' performance measurements aligned with their managers' decisions. The value creation index (VCI) is a measure of nonfinancial performance that was created to show the correlation between nonfinancial performance—essentially the impact from intangibles—and value creation. It measures the relative weight of nine nonfinancial drivers that affect value creation. The study revealed that the top three drivers are human capital intensive: (1) innovation, (2) the ability to attract talented employees, and (3) alliances.[26]

**The U.S. General Accounting Office (GAO).** As mentioned in Chapter 1, under the leadership of David Walker, the GAO is revamping its approach to human capital. The federal government is facing significant challenges in the coming years. The combination of cutting back new hires in recent years compounded by an aging workforce has resulted in a critical human capital turning point. Acknowledging past conduct, Walker comments that "the anecdotal evidence is that, in trying to save on workforce-related costs, agencies cut back on the training investments needed if their smaller workforces were to make up for institutional losses in skills and experience."[27] Based on its extensive study of nine private-sector companies, the GAO has summarized ten key principles of human capital management that form the foundation for the GAO's measurement practices. These tenets take a strategic approach to human capital management and development, beginning with the concept that human capital management is essential to strategic business management. They include factors related to hiring for competencies, using incentive compensation for individuals and for teams.[28]

The tenth principle speaks to the importance of measurement. The private-sector firms in the GAO study emphasized the importance of measuring human capital practices. The GAO learned about linkages between quantifying data and bottom line results as well as specific human capital strategies. It also observed that employees are more attuned to how their performance contributes to organizational success.[29]

**Interpretations of Federal Reserve statistics.** The Fed compiles a balance sheet of the U.S. economy. In 1998, it revealed that the country was worth approximately $40 trillion in intangible and financial assets. Michael Milken factored into the Fed's balance sheet people's expected earnings over the course of their life. Based on the financial models of Nobel Prize recipient Gary Becker, he extrapolated the value of human capital and concluded that the assets of the United States were actually worth between $180 trillion and $1 quadrillion in 1998, with human capital accounting for 75 percent of the total value.[30]

**Saratoga Institute.** Jac Fitz-enz, author of *The ROI of Human Capital: Measuring the Economic Value of Employee Performance,* is also the founder of the Saratoga Institute, a human capital research institute. Fitz-enz and his team of researchers studied retention issues by analyzing data from some 70,000 exit interviews for 50 companies. They concluded that when people join firms they expect to receive training and career support, have an opportunity to advance, be treated respectfully, have their knowledge put to use, have open lines of communication, and be compensated fairly. If any of these are missing, people become discontented. If several are not fulfilled, then they leave the company.[31]

Fitz-enz also created the formula for human capital return on investment. He concludes that companies with fewer than 500 people generate $1.68 in profits for every dollar spent on compensation and benefits. His method is based on dividing a company's compensation by an adjusted operating profit.[32]

**Watson Wyatt Human Capital Index.** This index, introduced in Chapter 1, measures the relationship between a firm's human capital and shareholder value creation. Specifically, Watson Wyatt, a human capital and financial management consulting firm, discovered that a significant improvement in 30 key human resources practices relates to a 30 percent increase in market value. It grouped these 30 practices into five dimensions, four of which revealed increases in market value from 1 standard deviation in improvement: recruiting excellence—10.9 percent; clear rewards and accountability—9.2 percent; a collegial, flexible workplace—7.8 percent; and communication integrity—4.0 percent. The last factor, prudent use of resources, had a counterintuitive 10 percent negative impact on shareholder value.[33]

## Moving from Theory to Practice

This chapter has introduced a number of policy and research studies, management tools, and specific examples of what firms are doing to measure intangibles, specifically human capital. The next step is to take this information from the theoretical to the practical. Companies will differ in terms of the measurements that they want to track and analyze. You may want to begin your process by performing a human capital audit. This will give you a lot of information on your people that you can use as a foundation for further assessment. A sample of such a review is in the Appendix.

Once you have performed your audit, take an objective look at the information. For example, are you facing high levels of attrition? If so, it is costing your firm a considerable amount of money to replace those workers. You may want to focus on increasing retention as a goal. To effectively analyze this, you will need to tap into your people to get a better sense of why so many people are leaving. Some of these conversations may be painful. If you are committed to creating value for the firm through your people, you have to ask the questions and pay attention to the answers. Start to make discrete changes that you can capture, record, and track. Over time, you will have enough information to conduct a thorough analysis to determine which tactics are contributing to higher retention.

Review the following ten-step checklist as a way to begin the measurement process. A sample case study is found in Figure 4.1.

1. Identify what you would like to measure. This could include any of the following:
   * Training and education
   * Incentive-based compensation or pay for performance
   * Turnover/retention
   * Leadership methods
   * Teamwork
   * Innovation and creativity
2. Once you have identified what you want to quantify, you need to break down the measure into components. Using incentive-based compensation as an example, you could monitor two parallel teams within the company that work on similar projects. One team would be the control group and would be paid salary as they have been paid in the past. The other

would be paid based on performance. You will need to quantify how the incentive pay will be quantified, for example:

FIGURE 4.1

## Crystalrose Housewares Case Study*

**Background.** Crystalrose is a privately held, high-end home furnishings company, specializing in customized bathrooms for upper-end homes. Crystalrose is launching a new product line and has set aggressive goals for its salespeople. The sales team consists of 45 associates covering major markets in the United States and Canada. The sales manager knows that her people can do the job but fears that motivation issues prevent optimal performance. Crystalrose has made the decision to invest in ongoing training and coaching for these salespeople, estimating the training will cost roughly $100,000. The company does not have this amount budgeted but made a decision to invest in the training based on specific outcomes.

**Target measurement.** Each of the salespeople has a goal of selling $750,000 of products, on average, over the course of a year, but additional incentives kick in when sales top $1 million. The average salesperson has been making $65,000 base salary and bonuses of $30,000 to 40,000 based on making goal; only three salespeople have been able to break the $1 million level. The sales manager set a goal that 18 of her people would reach the $1 million level as a result of the training.

**Strategy.** Training occurred in three phases. The first session included the entire sales staff, where they focused on the dynamics of their market and psychographic descriptions of their customers. They identified the ten most significant benefits of Crystalrose products and worked through the ten most frequently heard objections to buying the product. The second and third phases focused on smaller groups, where specific competencies were developed. All of the salespeople worked with a sales coach for six months to enhance their individual performance.

**Result.** The outcome of the training revealed that 4 of the salespeople elected to leave the company as the result of a mismatch of competencies. Of the remaining 41 people, 19 achieved the $1 million mark within two years. The incremental $4,750,000 of annual sales generated more than paid for the training as well as the additional incentive compensation that these salespeople received.

*Fictitious example based on actual companies.

- Finishing ahead of schedule
- Finishing on budget
- Finishing under budget
- Receiving additional business from the client as a result of the completed project
- Maximizing the talent on the team by attracting people from different areas of the company
- Using new innovations or methods in completing the project
- Maintaining strong internal reporting during the project

The list can go on—you can apply this example to any of the measures and derive a similar list. Of importance is that the measures are not necessarily about profitability or productivity. Using this example, the project team may have been rewarded by trying out and integrating a new technological innovation, which may be more important than coming in on budget. Only you know what is valuable for your firm. The important thing is to measure the information consistently so that you have systematic data to analyze.

3. After breaking down the data that needs to be captured, recorded, and tracked, make sure that your executive team agrees on the importance of the methodology. Buy-in is extremely important to the overall success of human capital measurements. It is more likely to happen, though, once you have laid some of the groundwork.

4. Create a linkage between the measurement and overall corporate goals. Make sure that successfully analyzing the data will be meaningful to your company.

5. Tie in your choice of measures to your corporate core competencies. The stronger the linkages between the measurement and what your firm does best, the more effective the outcome.

6. Do some external research to identify what other companies are doing—both within and outside your industry. Don't view this as a best-practices exercise. Instead, simply use it as research. Your corporate core competencies and your people are unique to your company, so best practices don't necessarily apply here.

7. Share your methodology with the people who are involved directly and indirectly with the data. Their buy-in will contribute to "owning" the results of the analysis.

8. Communicate the outcome of the project to everyone involved on a regular basis. Be open to suggestions for enhancing the process, no matter how seemingly unimportant the suggestion may be.
9. Make sure the process is dynamic. After you initially analyze the data, you may discover that you need either more or less information. You can alter the data gathering as long as the information being tracked going forward is consistent.
10. If your firm is publicly traded, start to share the information with analysts. This may be new information for them, but you can demonstrate leadership by stepping out ahead of the pack.

Identify what is important to your company—come up with measurements and apply them consistently. Using these measures will help you make better decisions. Although these are soft measures, by quantifying them, companies are able to speak the language of business. By quantifying nonfinancial data, managers will build the foundation from which they can decide how to allocate resources, when to hire new people, how to increase client satisfaction, and many other issues. Being able to quantify nonfinancial data means that you will compare apples to apples when making financial decisions. Laurie Bassi observes: "There's no way of getting around the fact that this is always going to be soft, but we can get at it in systematic, rigorous ways."

*O**NE SIZE DOESN'T FIT ALL*

**Make Your Own Rules**

*As seen by the case study in Figure 4.1, companies can customize measurements based on their specific needs. Start with one or two measurements and spend adequate time collecting and tracking the data before you analyze them. After you have created a foundation, you can move forward and analyze what you want when you want to. Remember that the measurements important to your company might not be the same measurements used by other companies.*

**Mergers, acquisitions, and divestitures.** Another practical application involves human capital implications if your firm is undergoing some type of consolidation. Performing a human capital audit is an effective way to appraise the value of the management of a new company to see if the cultures of the two companies mesh appropriately. In effect, you will perform a projected human capital profile of the combined company. Companies that value their people will understand the importance of this exercise, which is a much healthier approach than the traditional "us versus them" that typically occurs. The review will identify hidden strengths, barriers to success, availability of talent, and other areas of importance to the combined firm.[34]

The same concept applies in a divestiture. The human capital audit is essentially an inventory of the strengths and weaknesses of the collective group of people. A group of attorneys from a Denver-based law firm spun off into a new firm specializing in health care–related litigation. The partners identified their corporate core competency from the start. Each of the partners specializes in some aspect of the law—as well as some aspect of the business—so they had a balanced human capital revenue-generating team from the beginning. As the firm grows, it will review its position through the human capital audit to determine where they need to add people and how these people will create value for the firm.

## Final Thoughts

You've absorbed a lot of research and information from this chapter. It is a monumental task to measure something like human capital when there are no standards and few precedents to rely on. By capturing, recording, and tracking relevant data, however, you can create a system that will reap many benefits for your company over time. Chapter 5 examines more closely measures relating to attracting and retaining talent.

The key to successful development and implementation of human capital measurements is common sense. What is it that you want to track? Do you want to increase retention and decrease employee turnover? Do you want to measure customer satisfaction derived as a result of a new call center strategy? Would you like to evaluate the benefits of a new management training program? Identify what you would like to measure and what you will do with the measurement once you have enough data to analyze. Engage your people, your executive team, and your CPA to make this project a success. You will create the reality by taking a concept and turning it into a management tool that will enhance your firm's value in the future.

## CHAPTER RECAP

### Workplace Trends

- Companies are creating ways to measure their return on intangible assets.

- A company's intangible capital is an increasingly important contributor to shareholder value.

### Summary of Key Ideas

- Capturing, tracking, and recording data will result in a body of information that can then be analyzed to determine linkages. Ultimately, the goal of such measurements is to increase return on investment.

- The challenge in measuring intangibles, such as human capital, is that, by definition, they're not measurable.

- Many larger companies don't have significant internal reporting procedures in place, implying that they need to start from scratch to create systems to measure nonfinancial information.

- The differential between a company's book value and market value largely reflects the value of its intangible assets.

- The information that companies disclose to outsiders has a huge effect on what managers actually do internally.

- There is a need for standardizing measurements of nonfinancial information.

- Management tools that measure nonfinancial information have existed since the early 1990s and are variations on the "balanced scorecard."

- ASTD found that firms that invest more than average on training have significantly higher total shareholder returns.

- In its Capital Markets study, CBI found that 35 percent of portfolio allocation decisions were based on nonfinancial information, such as management experience, people's skills, and alignment with organizational goals.

- The GAO studied the practices of nine private-sector companies that measure human capital and summarized ten key principles that form the foundation of their measurement process.

## Thinking Points

- Review your internal reporting procedures to identify the data that your firm already tracks.

- Evaluate your firm's commitment to training and development and identify areas for improvement.

- Identify the top five nonfinancial measures that would provide meaningful information to your company.

- Create a plan to capture, record, and track data for one of these measures.

- Discuss concrete benefits of measuring nonfinancial data with your company's executive team.

# PART THREE

# How to Develop Human Potential in the Firm

*This last section is about attracting, retaining, and motivating your people. Firms that have the ability to recruit well have a definite competitive edge, an important ability regardless of the supply and demand of available people. Retaining people is another corporate competency. Given the high cost of replacing workers, your retention rate is an important nonfinancial measure to consider. The ability to diffuse limiting beliefs is as important in building potential as is technological savvy, both of which are addressed. Finally, the unique characteristics of leadership capital are examined.*

## CHAPTER 5

# The Art and Science of Attracting Talent

So how do you attract the best people for your firm? No doubt, you've heard a lot about the war for talent in recent years. A lot of people are baffled by the world of hiring. They just can't seem to find the right people. The frustration has led to a highly competitive environment (ergo, the "war" for talent), yet the way we hire people hasn't undergone the changes that you'd expect in such a competitive environment. Companies have hired a certain way for years, and no one has stopped to ask, "Why would there be value in changing?" Often, change is needed and you may benefit by approaching hiring from a completely different perspective than you have in the past.

In 1997, *McKinsey* delved into the war for talent by researching and surveying people in 77 large U.S. companies, concluding that companies can win the war for talent if they make talent management an absolute top corporate priority.[1] Moreover, *McKinsey* recommended you continually define why talent would want to work for you—the "what's in it for me?" factor. The survey revealed that only 23 percent of the 6,000 surveyed executives strongly agreed that their firms attract top talent. Part of the problem is that most companies don't define the attributes they want. Three years later, *McKinsey* updated its study and found that a whopping 89 percent think it's harder to attract talent and 90 percent think it's harder to retain talent. Of significance, it found that firms with the best talent management strategies are rewarded with higher shareholder returns, outperforming the mean by 22 percentage points.[2]

Attracting talent is a little bit of art and a little bit of science. There are specific, measurable actions that a firm can take to become a talent magnet. These are related to having an effective hiring strategy and measuring your success in recruiting and retention. The art of attracting talent relates to your corporate culture and reflects, in particular, how your firm values people. Companies that succeed in the art of attracting, retaining, and motivating top people will be rewarded by higher shareholder returns and lower attrition rates.

## Creating an Effective Hiring Strategy

There are several components to creating this strategy. Begin by clarifying your mission and philosophy. When you are clear about your corporate identity and the types of people you want, it is substantially easier to convey this information to people who don't know your company. This may seem obvious, but sometimes we can't see the obvious. Your firm may be shifting from a slow-growth to a high-growth mode. Clarifying your course during an accelerated period will obviously make a difference in terms of hiring requirements.

Next, outline your hiring objectives. Doing this will simplify the process greatly because it converts your philosophy into tactics. Identify how many people you will need to hire over fixed periods. Analyze the mix: Do you need full-time, salaried workers in the office, or will part-time, contract workers fulfill the goal? Evaluate your options and develop a plan.

Finally, make sure you have hiring policies in place in order to standardize and streamline processes. Policies include everything from benefits to probation periods to establishing clear goals and objectives.

### Your Hiring Philosophy and Mission

A hiring mission like "We hire talented people who bring our company to the next level" is so much of a platitude that it's almost a parody. How would anyone inside or outside of the organization know what kinds of people you are looking for? The example is so vague that people responsible to carry out the mission won't have a clue what they are supposed to do. This parody is actually improvised from an actual situation where the executives couldn't understand why their firm kept hiring the wrong people. They needed to metaphorically throw away that mission statement and reinvent the hiring process.

*Firms will attract employees who are a reflection of their corporate values.*

Start by aligning your hiring philosophy with your company values. If you value people who like to have fun, as Southwest Airlines does, for example, then this should be part of your hiring philosophy. Take your corporate values and assign adjectives that describe the types of people you want to have sitting next to you. Come up with a short, intelligible description of your hiring philosophy.

Make sure that the statements are simple and easily understandable. Use the ten-year-old test: If you question whether something is comprehensible, ask a kid. If it is clear to the child, you're probably in good shape. If it's not clear, the child will probably ask a question that goes to the heart of what you're trying to achieve. Some sample statements:

- "We hire top performers who are smart, people-oriented, life-long learners."

- "We hire achievers who love to sell."

- "We hire meticulous analysts who care about detail and accuracy."

- "We hire people who can make decisions and generate results quickly."

Notice how different those statements sound from the vague example —the parody. Figure out those you'd like to hire and create a statement that expresses it clearly and succinctly.

## Hiring Objectives

Essentially, your goal is to attract the best people with the right skills who can create maximum value for your firm, a goal that assumes a mix of talent and labor. You need to earmark how much you will invest in your new hires. Why not take it a step further and identify what type of return on investment you expect to receive from the people you hire? Some of these returns will be easier to quantify than others, but if we are using measurements as a way to quantify how productive your human capital is, the hiring process is the place to start.

**Analyzing the hiring mix.** In some cases, you will not need to invest in talent. The available positions may require people with certain skill-based competencies. The way to make the distinction between this type of labor and talent is easily understood by answering this question: "If Greta leaves this job in 18 months, will someone be able to easily pick up where she left off?" Generally, the answer is yes for lower-level or more labor-oriented positions. If a person leaves, someone else can take over relatively quickly. On the other hand, if you hire primarily engineers whose intellectual capacity contributes to your firm's revenue growth, then you're obviously investing in talent.

Most companies need both types of people. The lower-level jobs are classified more as labor, but a note of caution. People in lower-level positions are essential to your firm's success. They must be treated with the same respect you'd use to treat a rocket scientist. Successful management of people in lower-level positions often comes about from showing them the link between their job and the success measurements of the firm. For example, if a shipping clerk understands that impeccably packed and promptly shipped packages are one of her firm's trademarks, she will see a link between her role and value creation. Giving people a clear understanding of how their job fits within your firm's value chain is one of the biggest self-motivators there is.

❝ *Giving people a clear understanding of how their job fits within your firm's value chain is one of the biggest self-motivators there is.* ❞

## Creating Measurements

In Chapter 4, you became familiar with some of the measurements that can be used in human capital management and development. This section identifies recruiting-specific measurements that you can begin to assemble and implement immediately. As you capture data, keep in mind that you ought to collect it on both salaried employees and free agents. Unless you have been gathering this information already, it will take some time until you have enough information to analyze. Most firms do keep records of hire and departure dates of their salaried employees, but often no records are kept on independents.

Your biggest challenge may be the ability to access your central computer system for either adding fields or conducting analyses. In such a case, you will have to keep a separate accounting of necessary information. If the numbers are manageable, you can easily track them on standard spreadsheet software.

Be patient with the process. You may not have enough information to analyze for a while unless you can reconstruct it historically and analyze from historical data. Typically, you will have some of the information (such as hire and departure dates), but often other information doesn't exist.

Continue gathering information after you've come to some preliminary conclusions. Economic cycles, demographic factors, and other social issues can affect the numbers over time. The important thing is to *systematize a process* and consistently accumulate data that are analyzed at regular intervals. Please review Figure 5.1, which is the case study of a company with attrition issues. In addition, the following are examples of measures that will help you evaluate your recruiting efforts.

**Where do your best people come from?** You may recruit from a wide variety of venues, including colleges and graduate schools, trade associations, print and Internet advertising, recruiters, employment agencies, or referrals from other employees. While this may seem like an overwhelming task, it will generate some very important information. Here are the data categories that are important:

- Hire dates

- Departure dates

- General age range

- How employees heard about your firm

Once you have enough information, you can analyze employees' length of service and compare it to where they heard about your firm. Over time you will find interesting patterns. You may find that your best people mostly come through referrals from other employees. Tracking the general age range is important because you may see demographic patterns that are interesting. Your best Gen X workers, for example, may come from a particular source. After you've had a chance to analyze this information, you will be able to fine-tune your recruiting strategy so that you put more emphasis on where you're getting the best results. Remember the 80–20 rule— You get 80 percent of your business from 20 percent of your customers. It applies to recruiting as well as business development.

**FIGURE 5.1**

## Kissel Software Case Study*

**Background.** Kissel Software is a privately held, growth-oriented software development company with products in the growing children's reading market. Although it has ridden the ups and downs of the dot-com boom, it is on course for growing revenues at a rate of 20 percent per year. Based on Kissel's market position, reputation, and clientele, it is possible that the company can reach this growth if it takes a proactive approach to human capital management. Its biggest issue has been turnover, particularly that of bright, young employees, who tend to get experience at Kissel and then move on to other firms. Kissel conservatively estimates that the cost of replacing these employees is around 1.3 times an employee's annual compensation, or $45,000 each.

**Target measurement.** Kissel wants to decrease its attrition rate from 20 percent to 12 percent over a three-year period. In 2000, for example, Kissel had 100 employees in the category of bright, young employees, of whom 20 by year-end had left for other positions. This equates to $900,000 to replace the people who left. By reducing attrition to 12 percent, the company can save approximately $450,000 based on the 2000 employment levels. As the company grows and the number of people in the targeted category increases, the cost of attrition escalates.

**Strategy.** Kissel instituted three basic strategies to decrease the attrition level. First, it evaluated the job positions involved to determine the competencies necessary for success. Second, through diagnostics and staff review, it began to hire people who were a better fit in these positions. Third, it began conducting exit interviews to determine the reason why people were leaving.

**Results.** After one year, attrition has declined by four percentage points to 16 percent. The savings of $180,000 underestimate the actual savings, as one of the outcomes is the creation of new client-servicing positions as a result of feedback from exit interviews. The company believes that it also sold an additional $1.2 million in product based on the effectiveness of people in the new positions. These people have been compensated for their outstanding efforts, and their team is being modeled elsewhere in the company.

---

*Fictitious example based on actual companies.

**Increasing retention.** Most firms want to decrease turnover and increase retention. You will need to capture data that you may not currently obtain consistently with measurement in mind. Here are some key categories to capture:

- Hire dates

- Dates of departure

- Data collected from exit interviews as to why the person left the firm

- Would you rehire this person?

- Contact information (including address, phone, and personal e-mail)

Exit interviews are rarely conducted. An employee typically signs some papers, and that marks the end of his or her career at a company. The immediate manager may have more in-depth knowledge about why someone leaves, but that information is not nearly so accurate as a nonthreatening, confidential exit interview. During the exit interview, you want to learn what the person liked about working at the firm and what he didn't like. Over time, you ought to be able to gather some informal information about the firm that isn't immediately obvious on a day-to-day basis. Ideally, exit interviews ought to be conducted by an outside person who is not likely to be as biased as a company employee.

Some people may leave because they are relocating to another city. If your company has a presence there and you were pleased with this person's performance, you have lost if you didn't explore a transfer. If the person didn't raise the subject of a transfer with his or her manager, it suggests that either he or she was unhappy in the job or didn't trust the manager. Either way, you'll want to know why. Piecing together this kind of information can lead to some remarkable discoveries.

66 *The important thing is to systematize a process and consistently accumulate data that are analyzed at regular intervals.* 99

**What employees want.** You don't want to wait until your people have left to find out what didn't work for them. Why not create an employee survey that can be easily administered through your company intranet or by e-mail? Make it short and easy to complete so they don't put it aside. Have you ever received a customer satisfaction survey that was so long and complicated that there is no way you'll be willing to take an hour to complete it much as you like the vendor? Think of this when surveying your people. Keep it simple:

- What do you like about the work you do?

- What don't you like about the work you do?

- What do you like about working here?

- What don't you like about working here?

- What are the top three things that you would like to see us do differently?

Remember, the questions need to be nonthreatening. Until you have established trust around your intentions, you may need to have an independent entity administer the survey. If your people see that you are listening *and* making discrete changes that reflect their survey answers, you will be able to eventually bring the process in-house.

## Creating Standards and Procedures

Do you pay huge signing bonuses? Will you investigate the person? Does your firm obtain background checks and drug tests for everyone who is offered a job? Will you hire a person who doesn't have the proper immigration papers? Are these practices written in a policy manual, or do you make up new rules every time you hire someone?

Review your hiring manual, and if you don't have one, it's time to create one. Have an employment attorney review it to ensure that it includes all of the necessary information germane to your company and is in compliance with current employment law. It helps to have an attorney who specializes in employment on your team. Larger companies have them on staff. Smaller companies can outsource but make sure that the attorney is a specialist in employment law. Your regular corporate attorney isn't going to be your best resource if you have a problem because employment law is so specialized, especially state jurisdictional issues.

An *effective hiring manual* is an important document because of the litigious nature of our society. People threaten to sue for any imaginable reason. Most frivolous lawsuits go nowhere but still require employers to spend money on legal advice. Not only do you need to have standards and procedures in place when hiring people, you also need to make sure that compliance continues once a candidate is officially an employee of your company.

As an example, a middle manager was fired on the basis of sexual harassment by Miller Brewing Company. Not able to collect damages under wrongful termination, he filed a tort action claiming that the company had "misled" him by assuring him his career was on an upward path; he received $26.6 million in damages. The premise of the case holds bosses "liable for deliberately deceiving employees in a way that damages their careers."[3] Having a procedure in place will protect you if your company finds itself in a precarious position. A number of new, creative lawsuits are being filed against companies as well as individual managers. These types of lawsuits can exterminate a company, so taking the time to create policies and procedures is one step away from such lawsuits.

Decide when you will make exceptions to your standards and procedures. For example, will you hire Joe's neighbor without the regular interview process because Joe is your best employee and you trust him implicitly? It's hoped you won't. Shortcuts in hiring typically don't have a happy ending. Many hiring mistakes take place when employers are anxious about filling a position and are determined that the new hire will work out just perfectly. Unfortunately, such thinking often backfires.

Do you rely on your candidate's résumé and interview responses to be accurate? Résumé accuracy is one of the biggest deceptions in the hiring process. Falsifying responses in interviews has become an art form with some candidates. Some have become so proficient with their stories that they don't consciously know they are lying. A security company surveyed over 10,000 applicants in financial services and information technology and discovered that 25 percent of the candidates weren't telling the truth.[4]

You want to systematize the process of verifying résumé information. The more you automate the routine pieces of the process, the more efficient the system. Think about putting your application online, for example. Further, a person's demonstration of skill-based competencies, if needed, could also be done online. Once the person has gone through these initial steps, interviews can be scheduled on an automated online calendar. The screening process, then, becomes streamlined. It adds objectivity to the process, and, of greater significance, your people aren't wasting a lot of administrative time on the process.

What does the interview process look like? How many people will the candidate meet with? Will the person interview over a cross section of departments? How do you perform reference checks? How do you dig beneath the noncommittal responses from former employers that only verify dates of employment?

Will you use assessments to identify how candidates conduct themselves in the workplace and what motivates them to perform? At what point in the process do you introduce the assessment process? How do you use the assessments in the decision process?

Once the decision to hire is made, do you have a standard letter of engagement? If the person is brought on as an independent contractor, does the person sign a disclaimer in which she acknowledges her responsibility to pay income taxes? Do you have a customary probation period during which the candidate's performance is evaluated?

Do you have procedures in place related to promotions, raises, bonuses, and other compensation practices?

## The Hiring Quandary

Prospective employees want to do meaningful work in a pleasant environment where they feel valued for their contribution. They want to work for good managers and under strong leaders. That's the easy part. The hard part is when one of these factors is missing. Then all bets are off. One person is more driven by money while someone else wants job security. One wants work-life balance while another is a superachiever and is only happy leaping over tall buildings.

### *O*NE SIZE DOESN'T FIT ALL

#### *What Is Most Important in Recruiting?*

*Because power has shifted from employer to employee, recruiting can be a hugely complex process. So what is most important? Generally speaking, the answer depends on the stage of a person's career. Younger workers tend to want interesting work and career advancement. Midcareer people seek professional satisfaction, and older workers may be more security conscious. In all cases, people want to feel that they are treated fairly and valued. The word value is where interpretation creeps in.*

**Role models.** *Fortune* has showcased the 100 best American companies to work for for the past several years. The 1999 survey revealed that investments in employee education and training were important along with important "soft" benefits.[5] The 2000 survey showed that the best companies were offering everything from concierge services to flexible schedules to stock-based incentive plans.[6] The 2001 survey revealed more of the same, including a sampling of such perks as on-site day care, concierge services, domestic partner benefits to same-sex couples, and sabbaticals.[7] Companies that appear on this list attract better people and deliver enhanced returns to their shareholders.

## *W*ORKPLACE TREND

*Companies that offer a corporate culture of respect, along with interesting work, have a greater ability to attract talent.*

**Compensation.** As we move into a more talent-based employment world, talent will state its price for hire and the employer can decide if it will work. Of great importance, talent isn't looking just for money. Talent looks for ways to add meaningful work to its portfolios. Talent looks for opportunities to expand and grow. So money isn't necessarily always the only driver.

In spite of how pay ranks in a worker's priorities, pay for performance is increasingly important. Watson Wyatt's ongoing study of worker attitudes, *WorkUSA*, indicates that only 30 percent of workers feel there is a connection between pay and performance.[8] Visionary companies are experimenting with different types of incentives. Optimally, incentive compensation should include components of base salary, a share in the firm's ongoing profitability, and an opportunity to benefit from the upside through equity ownership. Even hourly workers, who are not typically knowledge workers, can become more committed to their job through meaningful incentives. These workers can contribute ideas on improving operating efficiencies, for example, and be paid a percentage of the savings as incentive. This compensation engages them more actively on the job and results in a commitment to production efficiencies.

*Incentive compensation* is one of the most direct ways to show appreciation to people. Workers in firms that provide some sort of pay for performance tend to work harder and are more committed to team and company goals. When people feel valued, they will work harder to achieve their goals.

**Benefits and perks.** At the peak of the dot-com boom, it seemed as though technology companies were trying to outdo each other with new benefit offerings to entice workers. Whether it was access to a driving range or free lunches or dog walking services, if you were a desired worker, you could demand the perk of your choice.

Today, a tight market for talent remains, but the offerings have come back to earth. Medical benefits, company matching in 401(k) plans, additional vacation time, and opportunities for advanced learning or training are among the most requested. A variation on defined contribution 401(k) plans is defined contribution health plans, which permit an employer to provide a specific amount of money for each worker's health benefits. Workers then buy plans that fit within this amount or pay the difference for a more robust health care offering.[9]

It is important that members of Gen X and Gen Y are more focused on balancing work-life issues than are their older colleagues. They may be willing to trade salary for benefits that give them more options for balance. Also keep in mind that once you provide "special" perks, it's harder to take them away. If a perk makes people feel special, discontinuing it may be interpreted as punishment. Perks are perceived as a statement that a company values its workers. With relatively little investment, firms can have a tremendous positive impact on the morale and attitude of their people.

**Workers as owners.** The bottom line is that if you want your people to have the gusto to grow your firm as if they owned the place, you need to give them a piece of it. This means a share of the equity that they can benefit from today, not options that won't be exercised until some time in the distant future. Options may be part of the compensation, but an ownership share is what matters.

Starbucks is a good example of a growing company that has successfully offered stock ownership across its employee ranks. UPS recently went from being a privately held company to a publicly held company. In the process, the majority of its workers became owners. For this strategy to be successful, your people need to specifically understand how the performance of their job contributes to the company's value creation.

Employee stock option programs (ESOPs), or broad-based stock option programs, are plans in which more than 50 percent of full-time employees receive options. These plans have become increasingly popular among privately held companies, particularly those whose revenues are based on intangibles. A Rutgers University study revealed that a 16 to 18 percent increase in productivity occurred in companies after stock options were issued.[10]

## Corporate Culture

Corporate culture is by far the most significant determinant of employee satisfaction. It is also the most elusive and the most difficult to explain. Corporate culture is the outward reflection of a company's values. If a corporate culture values people, compensation and benefit issues take care of themselves.

You can't recruit people by telling them that you have a great corporate culture. People have to experience it. Obviously, they are never going to know fully what it's like on the inside until they work there, but a company with a strong people-valuing culture is something that you experience from your first contact on the telephone or with a receptionist. Some of the best recruiters are your people. A testimonial from the inside is more valuable than any advertising campaign.

**❝ Corporate culture is by far the most significant determinant of employee satisfaction. ❞**

Similarly, candidates can immediately sense toxic working environments. Aside from the tension you can feel when you speak with people in toxic environments, leaders in these companies expect their people to work like indentured servants. Work is their life and life outside of work is secondary. Basic respect and common courtesy are rarely seen. People look over their shoulders because they don't know when they're going to get stabbed in the back—the antithesis of a culture that attracts talent.

A classic example of toxic leadership was Al Dunlap, who last appeared in corporate America as the CEO of Sunbeam Corporation. "Chainsaw Al," as he was known, was famous for his slash-and-burn techniques. He successfully eliminated significant numbers of workers from Scott Paper, Diamond International, and Lily-Tulip before he ever stepped foot into Sunbeam. There, he outdid himself, announcing sales of business lines and layoffs of a shocking 50 percent of the staff. A CEO or executive team that has no regard for people will attract workers who are fearful and timid. In the long term, it is a losing strategy as it strips the heart and soul from the firm. Sunbeam's board fired Dunlap in 1998, but unfortunately it was too late to make amends for his actions. The company is dealing with the aftershocks of Dunlap's management as it is now reorganizing under Chapter 11 of the bankruptcy laws.

You may wonder who would work for a company like Sunbeam under the leadership of someone like Dunlap. Who? Plenty of people because they are promised security or interesting work or advancement. Sometimes they don't have a choice or are afraid to look for another job. Others don't know that it's different anywhere else. Others work in companies under leaders like Dunlap because they get paid a lot of money. The seduction of money and the promise of a pot of gold at the end of the rainbow are the inducements. People knock themselves out for the reward du jour, and then they start over again in search of the next prize.

Companies whose cultures value people may not be the high-fliers. Many of them are privately held or family-owned businesses; and most offer a sense of family even if they aren't family owned. The feeling is one of inclusiveness and being valued. People who work for these companies know how they create value. The following examples reflect a cross section of company size and industry to illustrate positive corporate culture:

- The SAS Institute, the world's largest privately held software company, has gone against the Silicon Valley grain by providing a good work environment and a culture that promotes work-life balance instead of stock options. The company has a variety of perks, including on-site childcare and recreation facilities. The company discourages people working longer than a 35-hour workweek, which definitely goes against the grain of other companies in the software industry.[11]

- An ice cream maker and retailer in a Cape Cod village is known not just for great ice cream, but for the terrific people who work there at the height of the summer tourist season. The secret? The owner recruits accomplished students to work there by invitation. They become a member of an extended family and often work from the age of 16 through college.[12]

- Unimerco, a Danish engineering company, is an employee-owned company where the employees receive a share of the profits monthly. The company's managing director, Kenneth

Iverson, feels that engaging workers is a fundamental strategy that has a positive impact on the company's growth record. He comments that the employees think like small business owners and have greater buy-in as a result of their ownership structure.[13]

- The Container Store, ranked first in *Fortune*'s 100 best companies survey, has no gimmicks or perks to speak of. Its objective is to treat people well, and the rest will take care of itself. The company offers ongoing training and also has an open-book policy about sharing its financials. The results? In an industry that experiences 73.6 percent turnover annually, The Container Store clocks in at an impressive 28 percent.[14]

- Slimline, Ltd., a British-U.S.-Sri Lankan joint venture, produces lingerie for Victoria's Secret. Based in Sri Lanka, it attracts university graduates into management ranks. The firm has state-of-the-art technology and an ergonomically advanced environment for its 1,400 plant workers. The plant manager has the mandate to do what's necessary to make it work. The workplace structure is egalitarian, uncommon in Sri Lanka.[15]

The common theme among these stories is a positive work environment. Each company goes about it a little differently, yet the end result is that the work environment makes a difference in the ability to attract and retain productive employees. An attractive corporate culture increases retention and magnetizes other good candidates. The savings from decreased attrition and more effective recruiting drop straight to your bottom line.

# Ending the Relationship

## Layoffs

Inevitably, people leave. Sometimes it's a mutual decision. Other times, organizational issues may be insurmountable. Layoffs, downsizings, restructurings, voluntary reduction in staff—all affect workforce transiency. And all of these are laden with emotion. Usually the circumstances don't matter—the outcome is that people feel betrayed when they are let go.

A number of organizations make the mistake of laying off people at the first sign of trouble. This is bad policy. If business is so bad that the knee-jerk reaction is to lay off staff, then the company is making a highly unappealing statement. It is anchoring an image of not valuing its people and is one of the reasons why workforce transiency has increased so substantially. Workers feel there is no loyalty, as they could be laid off at the first sign of trouble. Rather than continue to subject themselves to this treatment, they opt for free agency.

More bad blood occurs when companies lay off people and then bring them back as independent contractors. Clearly the intent is to eliminate the firms' responsibility to pay benefits to these people. Such conduct does not build a sense of valuing your people; resentment grows and erupts at some point. Moreover, disgruntled ex-employees feel no hesitation to broadcast their dissatisfaction about these companies on the Internet.

Quitting is on the rise. There is a national quit rate, which is the percentage of people who are unemployed because they voluntarily left their job. Today, the average worker goes through about nine jobs by the age of 32. Quitting once a year is not unusual for people in the high-tech industry. As workforce transiency becomes the norm, quitting no longer has the stigma that it once had.[16]

Organizations that want to maintain employee goodwill are wise to make job cuts as humanely as possible. They can give employees time to leave in a dignified manner and provide support to them during the transition process. Although outplacement services are typically available only to senior people, companies can mimic the process by providing help at all levels. Assistance in career changes, job counseling, résumé writing, and interview skills are examples. Firms that take the time to disengage staff with dignity are likely to be remembered favorably when they are again hiring.

**❝ Organizations that want to maintain employee goodwill are wise to make job cuts as humanely as possible. ❞**

Effective communication is essential in layoff situations. When layoffs occur as a surprise, it creates bad blood, no matter what the reason. Your company's leadership will be blamed, and your former employees will waste no time in telling others that your company is not a good place to work. The situation is exacerbated by the Internet, where people feel free to post their opinions electronically so even more people can read about them.

## Voluntary Resignations

People resign voluntarily for personal and professional reasons. Retirement or relocation are two easily understandable reasons. Some people leave because they feel they no longer have opportunities to grow within your firm. This may be true. You won't be able to hold on to your employees forever, nor should that be a goal. The question: Are you losing talent for "legitimate" reasons, or is talent leaving because it doesn't feel valued in your company?

This may be hard to evaluate. Many firms have an attitude of "good riddance" when good people leave. That attitude is more likely a cover-up for lack of awareness that a problem exists. If your company is losing talented people on a regular basis, it's time to take a look at why. Granted, it's easy to take good people for granted, but taking them for granted over time isn't the best course of action.

# Rehiring

After the dot-com bubble burst, many of the people who left traditional firms to work at dot-coms went back to their former employers looking for a job. Although many of these companies gladly welcomed back former colleagues, others have had more skeptical attitudes. It's worthwhile to establish a policy about rehiring. The nature of workforce transiency is such that talent rehires will occur more frequently even without the influence of dot-coms.

Companies can be creative when they must cut staff but know they will need to rehire. A bakery that supplied bread to major hotel clients in lower Manhattan was directly affected by the terrorist attacks on the World Trade Center. Rather than lay off its workers, this family-owned business asked its workers to take a voluntary reduction to a four-day workweek until business returned to more normal volume. A voluntary reduction in time is a reasonable solution when you know the situation is temporary. Workers tend to take a short-term cut in pay to stay with a company they like. Some family-owned businesses offer employees the choice to vote on voluntary reductions versus layoffs. This gives workers a sense of participating in the process rather than receiving a mandate from above.

Brokerage firm Charles Schwab asked its workers to voluntarily take Fridays off at the beginning of the most recent economic downturn. Later, when the firm had no choice but to lay off people, it offered a $7,500 bonus to any laid-off worker who is rehired within 18 months. Cisco proposed an unusual option to its workers. Instead of a severance package, Cisco employees could continue receiving benefits, stock option awards, and one-third of their normal salary if they worked for a nonprofit chosen by Cisco. There are no guarantees that Cisco will rehire them, but the plan is a way to hedge bets on both sides. Accenture offered voluntary sabbaticals to its U.S. consultants. Texas Instruments took a different approach by "lending" several hundred employees to vendors for up to eight months.[17]

## Alumni Networks

Companies are actively establishing alumni networks to help in finding talent. For example, former employees of large consulting firms can tap into their network of colleagues. As reported in a *Fast Company* article, Bain & Company communicates with its alumni more often than most companies communicate with their current employees.[18] Staying in touch with former employees is an excellent way to stay "top of mind." It is in your best interest to do so, because at some point your former employees may become clients—or refer clients—to your firm.

Creating an alumni organization is an excellent way for your organization to formally extend a relationship with people who no longer work for you. Even if your company is small or midsized, or doesn't experience a lot of turnover, keeping people connected will ultimately bring value to your firm. Alumni can become your clients. They can refer clients. They can refer employees. They can tell your story and support you in the marketplace. Former employees can be tremendous advocates for your firm. Of most importance, perhaps, they know how you treat human capital, and word gets around. Think of this as a way to create lifetime advocates of your company.

### WORKPLACE TREND

*Cultivate relationships with your people so that they are* lifetime advocates *of your firm.*

Creating an alumni organization works splendidly if people had great experiences while affiliated with your firm. If they felt valued, if you provided them an opportunity to develop their potential, if you supported them with their decision to move to a position outside of your firm, they will be lifetime advocates for you. On the other hand, if their experiences were lackluster or negative, then you've missed an opportunity to have someone speaking well on your behalf. Even worse, employees' negative experiences can convert into complaining about your firm and potentially damaging your reputation.

    **66** *Creating an alumni organization is an excellent way for your organization to formally extend the relationship with people who no longer work for you.* **99**

## Matching What You Want with What "They" Want

You can see why it is important to begin with a clear hiring philosophy and strategy. There is so much focus on what people want from their employers that your firm's objectives can get lost in the discussion. An effective recruiting strategy not only saves money in the long run (through reduced attrition) but attracts top-quality people who enhance the value of your firm's human capital. Here are some thoughts about how you can approach recruiting:

- Hire the right person for the position by assessing the job first. Objectively assess the requirements of the job—without bias— and then recruit a candidate who has credentials that match the job. Here's an example. You need several salespeople and hire terrific go-getters who love to meet with clients and develop business, but they fail. Had you looked at the job objectively from the beginning, you would have identified customer service skills as the most important competency for this job. Clients only want to be sold to if someone will take care of them afterward. Hiring the wrong people can be a costly mistake, when you don't properly evaluate the position.

- Look outside your industry for ideas. Never been in the military? Then maybe learning how the U.S. Marines recruit the best candidates can help. Master Gunnery Sergeant Andy Brown has three suggestions. First, have your best people recruit if you want to hire the best candidates. Second, look for what motivates a person and how that can apply in your organization. Third, look for commitment and accountability.[19]

- Just as we cultivate spheres of influence when we are engaged in business development, we can do the same when recruiting. If you hire someone who is well respected by her peers and direct reports, this person might be a magnet for other people to join. Of course, the flip side is that if the person is not happy in your company, she and her cohorts will find a new place to bring their talent.

- Hire for potential. People may not have all of the skills, but if they have the potential and you are willing to provide the learning environment, it should be a win-win for both parties. The person will feel valued because you believed in him and you will benefit from extracting previously untapped value.

- If your company is taking bold steps to get ahead, consider hiring people who have experienced failure. Failure and the resiliency that follows can be a great motivator. Considerable benefit can result from recruiting someone who graduated from the school of hard knocks. The person is probably more comfortable taking risks, especially knowing that you are aware of his past experiences.

- Consider the vast number of people who are reinventing themselves. People entering the workforce today are likely to have up to nine different careers in their lifetime. Think about how the person's prior work experience applies to what you are offering. And of particular importance, identify whether the person's competencies fit what the job needs. If there is a match, go for it.

- If you don't know the life expectancy of a particular position, hire a long-term temp from an agency. Increasingly, companies hire for projects that extend from one to six months. Temp agencies aren't just for administrative people any more. Many temp agencies specialize in areas ranging from accounting to project management to marketing. They take care of payroll taxes, benefits, and other tasks that make a short-term hire more problematic.

- Offer referral fees to employees who introduce people who are hired. Eighty-three of *Fortune*'s 100 best companies offer referral fees, including a $15,000 referral fee at three of the companies.[20]

## People as "Tradable" Capital

As the free agent model becomes more prevalent, employers will become more accustomed to paying talent on a market basis. There are interesting pay-for-performance variations on this theme. For example, if you hire people to work on a project, pay them a base wage *and* a share of the profitability of the project as it comes on stream. Rather than providing equity in the company, you are essentially providing equity in the project. You can do this with salaried employees as well as independents. The point is that you're giving all of them the opportunity to bet on the upside of their projects.

Privately held firms use profit sharing or ESOPs to provide incentives to their workers. A midsized accounting firm created a phantom stock program to simulate its value in the stock market. Participants have to invest an initial amount to participate but are able to make additional investments annually. They are guaranteed a minimum return, but the value of the shares is based on the firm's cash flow.[21]

MacTemps (now Aquent) acts as a talent broker, matching companies with talent. The people who apply to be "listed" at MacTemps go through a formal evaluation process before they are accepted. Many of them are specialists in areas ranging from software applications to graphic designing to Hypertext Markup Language (HTML). MacTemps acts more as a talent agency than an employment agency, meaning that the business is geared to the talent.[22]

A number of expert sites have emerged on the Internet to serve the free-agent market. Unlike MacTemps, however, the people are not vetted. On most of these sites anyone can list himself as an expert in anything from employment law to outsourcing CFOs to Web design. Many offer a rating feature similar to one you see on eBay, so purchasers have a sense of who they're buying. Remember that on the Internet you never know with who you may be communicating. In *Next,* Michael Lewis talks about the youngster who was the top-rated attorney on one of these sites. No one knew he was a kid.[23]

## Final Thoughts

You have explored both the art and science of recruiting. It will be worthwhile to establish concrete recruiting and retention measurements as a way to analyze where you're getting the best talent and how to keep them longer. It is also important, though, to take a look at what is unique about your corporate culture and how it can be a means to attract and retain talent. If your corporate culture is nondescript, don't worry. You can create any image that you want. This will require buy-in across the ranks of your company, not just in words on paper but in the actions reflecting those words. Remember that more effective recruiting and retention have a positive cash impact on your company, as you are hiring better from the start and spending less to replace workers in the long run.

## CHAPTER RECAP

### Workplace Trends

- Firms will attract employees who are a reflection of their corporate values.

- Companies that offer a corporate culture of respect, along with interesting work, have a greater ability to attract talent.

- Cultivate relationships with your people so that they are *lifetime advocates* of your firm.

### Summary of Key Ideas

- To create an effective hiring strategy, clarify your mission and philosophy, articulate your hiring objectives, and ensure that hiring policies are in place.

- One of the best self-motivators is to give people a clear understanding of how their job creates value within your firm.

- Understand the inner dynamics of your work environment by conducting objective exit interviews of departing employees.

- Make sure you have a comprehensive policy manual for hiring staff.

- People look for different job-related experiences, largely depending on what stage of their career they are in.

- If you want your people to help you grow your company, you should give them some sort of equity.

- Corporate culture is by far the most significant determinant of employee satisfaction.

- Organizations that want to maintain employee goodwill are wise to make job cuts as humanely as possible.

- The nature of workforce transiency suggests that talent rehires will occur more frequently.

- Creating an alumni organization is an excellent way for your organization to formally extend its relationship with people who no longer work for you.

## Thinking Points

- Establish your recruiting philosophy and objectives in language that outsiders understand.

- Identify recruiting and retention measures that would benefit your firm.

- Establish a pilot program to capture, record, and track hiring-related and retention-related data.

- Evaluate your workforce to better understand what they seek by working for your firm.

- Describe your corporate culture. Ask for input from the most senior and least senior people in the firm.

## CHAPTER 6

# Organizational Capital

The Monteverde Cloud Forest Biological Reserve in northwestern Costa Rica is a majestic testimony to how ordinary people can practice conservation and maintain a protected environment. Because the environment is so fragile, only 100 people are admitted at a time. Once inside, you walk along the two-kilometer Cloudy Trail to the Continental Divide. Walking along this trail, even the most ignorant naturalists are awestruck by what they see, hear, and smell. More than 400 species of birds alone are in this reserve along with hundreds of species of plants and trees. The resulting biodiversity is represented in a series of interdependent ecosystems.

If you removed a three-wattled bellbird from the Cloud Forest and relocated it to the not-so-tropical island of Manhattan, it would die. This unique bird is meant to coexist in the Cloud Forest of Costa Rica, not the urban jungle of Manhattan.

Top-performing companies have ecosystems that operate like those in the Costa Rican Cloud Forest. They include groups of people who have come together to create products and services that are sold to businesses or consumers. Nature provides us with many blueprints for how organizations can function. These organizational structures, however, do not simply emerge from nature. They need to be consciously created and maintained to provide the optimal environment for work to be performed and for the workers to flourish.

Companies must provide an environment that gives their people the opportunity to develop and achieve their potential. Attracting talent and then just letting it fend for itself in a nonsupportive environment sets up talent for failure. Organizational capital provides the infrastructure and support that helps to enhance the value of your people, which in turn provides the foundation for achieving organizational goals.

> **❝** *Organizational capital provides the infrastructure and support that helps to enhance the value of your people.* **❞**

The mergers and restructurings that flourished in the mid-1980s led to the elimination of layers of middle management and massive layoffs of staff. The people who remained often performed one or two jobs in addition to their originally designated job. People pitched in and did whatever was needed, even though they may not have been qualified to do those additional jobs. Over time, people may have forgotten why they worked there, because they were no longer thriving in their core competency.

In times of expansive growth, more possibilities are afforded workers to do what they do best. During contractions, however, displacement occurs. Whether that means being laid off or being asked to do multiple jobs, displacement is a strain on the organization and disruptive for workers. People stay in these temporary jobs for indeterminate periods, but eventually, the temporary jobs become institutionalized, and workers feel permanently displaced. Managers don't remember that these employees were only supposed to be in those jobs for short periods.

The result is that many people feel they are "winging it." Being uncomfortable in their current job is just one piece of the puzzle. They don't understand the company's vision and mission—because it may have changed nine times since the beginning of the year. They don't have a sense of the corporate values and may be working out of alignment with what the company is trying to accomplish. They don't know what is expected of them. Job descriptions are vague and performance measurements don't exist. Some don't even know to whom they report. One banking executive was fond of saying, "If you see my boss, tell me his name."

This organizational turmoil affects how we develop talent. In the manufacturing era, people did their jobs and were evaluated by the output that their machines created. There were layers of supervisors and a fairly rigid structure of review and evaluation. Knowledge-based companies tend not to have these hierarchies. Workers are responsible for doing their job under the stated terms of employment.

Often, however, they are accountable for results without having the necessary authority to get the job done.

The new economy has resulted in the dismantling of corporate hierarchies. Older workers may seem frustrated or confused by these changes, whereas younger workers never knew the previous bureaucratic structure. This blurring of layers, combined with the shift in power from employers to workers, results in a workplace dynamic that is somewhat more fragile and untested.

## WORKPLACE TREND

*Value is now created at all levels within an organization, not just at the top layers.*

Value is now created at all levels within an organization, not just at the top layers. We must match the right people to the right positions, allowing their natural gifts to emerge and flourish. When this happens, it is more likely that workers will understand how they contribute to their firm's value. You will see buy-in across the ranks, giving the corporate ecosystem the chance to reach its potential. Training and education are important elements in enhancing the value of our people and contributing to overall organizational health.

## Dismantling the Hierarchies

Before the emergence of knowledge-based companies, higher-level managers and executives were perceived as the drivers of value creation. Their recommendations and decisions influenced the rate of growth for revenue and profitability. The emergence of knowledge-based companies, however, has seen a fundamental change; now workers at all levels contribute to value creation.

The breaking down of hierarchies is not universal; in fact, hundreds of companies still operate bureaucratically. New economy companies tend not to have bureaucratic structures, but each company must be evaluated individually. In some cases, a traditional bureaucratic structure enables high productivity. More likely than not, though, these companies would demonstrate improved efficiencies if they stripped away unnecessary layers. The fact that the federal government is disassembling its hierarchies and undergoing a massive human capital restructuring is testimony that old bureaucracies can reinvent themselves.

A number of factors have contributed to the disassembling of hierarchies. The elimination of layers of management, increased access to information, and the growth of technology are three key factors. Moreover, successful knowledge-based firms operate more as networks than as linear reporting structures. Processes and projects are managed rather than people.

## Elimination of Management Layers

Many organizations have significantly flatter organizational structures since the hierarchical dismantling began in the mid-1980s. It is significant that companies have eliminated more managers of people than managers of processes. Increasingly, managers oversee projects. Obviously, workers execute these projects, but people aren't being managed as directly as they were when multiple layers of management, whose sole responsibility was to supervise other workers, existed.

Flatter organizations have inherent challenges in that sometimes it is more difficult to identify final decision makers. This is where the accountability/responsibility dilemma arises. If a worker responsible for managing a customer service process identifies something that ought to be improved, he may not have the authority to make the change. With fewer obvious lines of responsibility, it may not be clear who can sign off on a request. Often, no one particular person is accountable for signing off, thus resulting in frustration over making a simple change.

Firms that organize on a matrix basis minimize this problem. Process and project managers know the appropriate organizational venues to find their answers. One manager may have primary responsibility for a functional area but may also have specific accountability for a companywide project. Roles are clearly articulated and, of equal importance, the corporate culture supports prompt decision making.

Top-performing companies go a step further by granting process and project managers the authority to make more substantial decisions. These could be earmarked by a dollar amount, for example, without the need to ask for additional approval. People who work in these firms tend to be more productive and feel more valued by their work. When you give people the responsibility and authority to do their job, the results can be exceptional.

**❝** *When you give people the responsibility and authority to do their job, the results can be exceptional.* **❞**

## Access to Information

As a result of much easier access to information, workers don't have to consult higher-level managers to find information. Some firms centralize information in such a way that workers can tap into systems to find answers that were previously known primarily by managers. If your company doesn't have a centralized knowledge bank, workers can tap into their informal network of contacts or research on the Internet to find the information.

Current worker access to information is an important shift. In hierarchical firms, senior managers were perceived as the authorities in their department. They "held the magic" by keeping their information close to the vest. This doesn't work today when a 12-year-old can find the same information through a simple Internet search. Access to information, then, has completely shattered the notion of senior manager as guru. The elimination of management layers and easier access to information happened concurrently. Together they contributed to dismantling the hierarchies.

**❝** *Access to information has completely shattered the notion of senior manager as guru.* **❞**

## Growth of Technology

The growth of technology has significantly influenced the dismantling of hierarchies. Aside from enabling access to information, it has also provided the means for automation. Mechanization has emerged on many levels, ranging from accounting systems to CRM (customer relationship management) software to distribution and logistics processes. As a result, the people responsible for execution are experts in their own right. They have been trained in the technology that makes the system work. If the technology doesn't work, the operator will likely reach out to the technical support help desk of the technology provider rather than asking an internal manager for help.

When updates or embellishments are added to the system, the technology provider trains your workers in the nuances of the enhancements. It is then your employees' responsibility to make sure that the internal applications of these upgrades are in alignment with overall company goals. As explored further in Chapter 8, maximizing the technology/human interface is an important way that firms can enhance the collective value of their human capital.

The growth of technology has been threatening to many executives who came from the manufacturing era. In the mid-1980s, the president of a major U.S. bank was horrified by the thought that personal computers were appearing on everyone's desk. Not only did he think it was ridiculous, but managers who allowed this to happen were reprimanded. The bank was subsequently merged into extinction but consider this mind-set: Technology made this executive uncomfortable; he didn't have the vision to see the possibilities; he didn't understand it; but most important, he wasn't able to "hold the magic" by withholding information from the public domain of his bank.

## Enter the Networked Organization

It doesn't matter whether your company is a retailer, a manufacturer, or a service business. Proprietary processes and ideas—often utilizing technology—are transforming firms into knowledge-based companies. If you retool your manufacturing process as a result of a technological innovation, for example, your company is becoming knowledge based. Your workers will be retrained as knowledge-based workers to maximize their productivity.

Networks are one of the elements that drive knowledge-based companies. If you visualize a map of the interstate highway system, you know that the interlocking connections occur at optimal places so that traffic can flow to its destination without going out of its way. The networked organization operates on the same idea. Instead of wading through layers of bureaucracy, people communicate directly to those who are best suited to contribute to the successful accomplishment of projects.

Networked organizations typically have self-managing project teams that function autonomously. Members of the team are responsible for achieving group goals and optimizing the workflow among its members. People perform well in these systems. They use their intelligence, skills, and experience to collectively achieve corporate goals—a good example of how human capital can contribute to a firm's prosperity.

> **❝** Networked organizations typically have self-managing project teams that function autonomously. **❞**

## Casualization of the Workplace

We used to be able to distinguish upper management from lower-level workers by their dress. Suit and tie were standard issue for all executives, no matter what type of firm. Today, even the most conservative firms have introduced a more relaxed dress code. You still see a lot of suits in investment banks and law firms, but there is generally a shift to more casual dressing.

Knowledge-based firms paved the way for this trend. The more casual high-tech companies in Silicon Valley set a new dress standard in the form of chinos and polo shirts. During the high-tech run-up of the late 1990s, investment bankers and venture capitalists who called on high-tech companies had to relax their style to connect with these clients. The Silicon Valley intelligentsia did not embrace the authoritarianism of navy blue suits and conservative striped ties.

## The Old "White and Blue"

We've used the expressions *white-collar workers* and *blue-collar workers* for years, classifications that emerged in the 1950s when William H. Whyte's *Organization Man* reigned supreme. White-collar workers used to be described as those who worked in office, professional, or managerial positions. Their jobs were distinguished from blue-collar workers mainly because they worked in offices instead of factories, but hierarchies existed within the white-collar domain. Lower-level employees were paid on an hourly basis, whereas middle-level and upper-level workers were salaried.

Blue-collar workers, on the other hand, were typically factory workers and laborers. Few had studied beyond high school. White-collar workers were perceived to hold a higher status, a standing granted because they tended to be better educated and worked more with their brains than their hands. Blue-collar workers tended to be hourly employees and didn't always receive company benefits. The compensation and benefits for white-collar workers were based on what the company mandated; workers had no opportunity to cut their own deals.

## Crumpling the Collars

One of the casualties of dismantled hierarchies has been the changing identity of both white-collar and blue-collar workers. When the service economy overtook the manufacturing economy, there was a proportionately higher increase in the number of white-collar workers. When restructuring, downsizing, and reengineering gained momentum in the 1980s, thousands of people were laid off. For the first time in history, however, white-collar workers were let go. Before, layoffs typically didn't affect them; only blue-collar workers would have been laid off. This trend rocked the personal foundation of many white-collar workers, as they had been brought up with the belief that their college education and hard work would protect them in the corporate setting.

As a consequence of this corporate betrayal, white-collar workers felt disloyal for the first time; they could no longer count on their job being secure. Loyalty from both sides became outdated quickly. The old paradigm of corporate paternalism cracked and rapidly fell apart in the coming decades. Gen Xers entered the workforce just as white-collar job security began to disintegrate. Their perspective has been one of distrust and suspicion from the beginning, while baby boomers and matures felt duped by the changed paradigm.

Growing corporate infidelity and dismantling of corporate hierarchies, then, were strong influences in the smudging of blue-collar and white-collar workers. Many blue-collar jobs were being enhanced by technology, therefore becoming more knowledge oriented. At the same time, some white-collar workers felt they were being treated unfairly and started to use traditional blue-collar methods, such as strikes, to make their point.

You might remember the movie *Network*, when Peter Finch leaned out the window and declared to all who would hear him, "I'm mad as hell and I'm not going to take it any more." This is happening with white-collar workers. They are no longer satisfied with the old status quo. If they are working 90 hours a week, they want to be paid for it. Worker-friendly labor laws in California, for example, have recently resulted in overtime for such white-collar workers as store managers and programmers.[1]

White-collar professionals in some old-line American multinationals have felt disenfranchised as a result of the increasing status of their counterparts at technology companies. A group of engineers at Boeing represented by their professional association, the Society of Professional Engineering Employees in Aerospace (SPEEA), were part of the largest white-collar strike in history. They protested compensation differentials between Boeing and Microsoft; differences in status and cost of living were at the core of the strike.[2] From doctors to graduate students to office workers, white-collar professionals are making their point by going on strike.

The Internet has enabled much of this activity. Workers use corporate intranets to communicate everything from policy to employee benefit changes. IBM employees used their intranet as a way for workers to collectively dispute proposed changes in IBM's pension plan. Workers at Bell Atlantic (now Verizon) assembled on the Internet to vote against changes in their pension plan that would have adversely affected longer-term employees.[3]

## *W*ORKPLACE TREND

*The Internet will increasingly be used as a vehicle for employee discussion and lobbying for benefits and compensation issues.*

Backlash is occurring across the ranks. In the past, executives didn't have to worry about white-collar unrest. Employees may not have liked what they were doing, but they did their job, no matter how long it took. Now it's different. And again a fundamental issue that companies need to address is how to treat their people as talent to be nurtured rather than labor to be taken for granted. Talent doesn't go on strike; it simply moves on to another position. More important, talent wouldn't be in the situation that would result in this sort of unrest.

&&*A fundamental issue that companies need to address is how to treat their people as talent to be nurtured rather than labor to be taken for granted.* ""

Treating your people as talent goes a long way to diffuse employee backlash. Your organizational capital provides the support and infrastructure that enables talent to thrive. It is important for your executive team to achieve buy-in on the issue of enabling talent to thrive. Otherwise, you run the risk of strikes or other backlash. Reduced to its simplest terms, a strike sends the clear message, "I don't feel valued." It is up to your firm to make sure this doesn't happen.

## Retooling the Blue-Collar Workforce

Blue-collar and white-collar positions as such will become increasingly obscure in the coming years. Companies that manage both types of workers need to understand the dynamics that may occur with each group and do their best to mitigate the fears and suspicions that may emerge. The solution begins with a corporate commitment to develop workers as talent, which includes enhancing the position of blue-collar workers as well. You may ask, can blue-collar workers be retooled into knowledge workers? The answer is yes, if your firm is willing to invest in training and education.

Companies with large constituencies of blue-collar workers must address the issue of retooling. Executives of publicly traded companies may have to make the painful decision to forgo the short-term demands of Wall Street in order to invest in retooling for transforming their workers from mechanized laborers into knowledge-economy workers who are comfortable with the demands of the 21st-century work environment.

### The Changing Face of Blue-Collar Workers

Blue-collar workers have also undergone changes in recent years. A disparity can be found between the GM factory employee who works in a technologically state-of-the-art manufacturing facility and his small-town factory counterpart. The GM worker may earn twice as much as the small-town worker, who doesn't have the same breadth of employment options. In fact, a limited economic situation exists in small towns, whose economy typically centers on a single manufacturing facility. Residents of these communities are victims of monopsony, where they are dependent on a single employer for work. The employers have a lot of clout by being the only game in town; and wages and benefits are often significantly lower, with few union options available.

Millions of blue-collar workers are found in back office or support centers. We may not automatically think of them as blue-collar because their "factory" is a customer service call center rather than an assembly line. Then, there is a vast contingency of unskilled laborers who are essential to the functioning of the economy. These people aren't usually thought of as blue-collar; often, they're simply forgotten.

One of the biggest challenges for blue-collar workers across all of these categories is the lack of room for upward mobility despite the adequate number of entry-level jobs that may be available. Some companies, then, take it as a fact of business life that people will just move on to other jobs. How do you keep a file clerk or a maintenance person motivated to stay in the same job? The solution is to either create upward or lateral mobility within the firm, or to change the value proposition of the position. If the file clerk understands how his or her job contributes to the bottom line, it could make a difference in how that person views the job.

ISS, the Danish support services group, has addressed this problem and has pioneered programs for its largely blue-collar workforce. It has decentralized power, for example, so that team leaders of cleaning crews are responsible for contract profitability. They are also responsible for customer satisfaction and employee training. ISS offers job mobility in countries like Norway and the opportunity to buy shares of ISS at a discount.[4]

Workplace improvement programs have evolved as a way that blue-collar workers can contribute ideas about improving efficiency. IBM was a pioneer in this area, offering financial incentives to workers who contributed ideas that enhanced productivity. The Bic Corporation, as another example, has a weekly meeting of hourly employees and management led by a blue-collar worker who functions as the employee-involvement administrator. The vast majority of Bic's hourly employees contribute ideas that are implemented. The workers' enthusiasm for this program isn't just about the money they receive as awards for ideas generated but even more about the sense of teamwork that has emerged.[5]

## The New Unions

Unions are undergoing fundamental changes as a result of workplace shifts. In 1979 there were 21 million union members, while in

2000 the number had dropped to 16 million. In the 1950s, 35 percent of workers belonged to a union compared with some 13.5 percent today.

Unions may be making a comeback, however, despite changed demographics, as a result of their effective use of technology and the Internet. Among other things, unions are becoming more democratized because of the Internet, which provides unions the opportunity to speak directly to workers about union policy and workplace issues without directly involving companies' management. Increasingly, unions will coordinate transnationally with labor organizations in other countries as a way to revitalize their efforts.[6]

It is unlikely that unions will regain the clout that they possessed in past years. Their comeback, however, may stem from using the communication vehicle of the Internet to lobby for worker retooling and education. Some 2,700 trade union Web sites already exist on the Internet, and this number is likely to increase. The newest players are e-Unions, virtual organizations providing a variety of services for workers that are similar to services affinity groups make available, such as legal advice or career assistance.[7] The growth of affinity group-cum-union is a way to provide services to constituents, particularly as the workers are transient. The e-Unions can fulfill their objectives simply because it's easy for workers to connect with them, no matter where they may be relocating.

## The Importance of Ongoing Workplace Education

Firms that believe their blue-collar workers are more than commodities can lead the way by providing training and other workplace education to enhance the value of these workers. Historically, blue-collar workers have not been targeted for training and educational opportunities, but this must change if companies want to change the value proposition for these workers. Providing educational opportunities will not only make them feel valued but will result in enhanced performance. Making education more accessible and desirable will result in a significantly more valued population of workers.

One of the biggest obstacles to the strategy of workplace education relates to attitudes about turnover. Many firms don't feel they should make training available as many workers are likely to leave after short periods of employment. On the contrary, by making training available, workers will likely feel more valued and self-empowered. Even if large numbers of workers do leave, companies cannot afford to be at a competitive disadvantage from their workers being poorly trained.

Another obstacle to blue-collar training is time. Workers don't have the incentive to take time for training and development because it requires them to be away from their jobs. Companies need to make training and education accessible by providing positive incentives to encourage workers to attend classes. If the workers don't see benefits from taking the training, why should they give up work time?[8]

Unusual alliances have been formed to address this issue of education. The Communications Workers of America (CWA) asked Cisco for help in retraining its workers, who enroll in the curriculum offered by Cisco's four-semester networking-academy program. The course work is primarily online and is supplemented by direct instruction and exams in a CWA regional training center. On completion of the program, CWA workers can upgrade into new positions. Cisco has trained an informal cadre of people who are now familiar with Cisco's perspective on computer networking, routers, and other Internet-related communications interfaces.[9]

Creative alliances have also appeared in the industrial sector. Manufacturing companies face the issue of hiring skilled workers, an increasingly shrinking labor segment. Small and midsized manufacturers in Pittsburgh collaborated with Duquesne University and a local foundation to create Manufacturing 2000. This training program targeted career-oriented people who found themselves in dead-end jobs. The program trains them to become machinists, welders, and other industrial labor specialists.[10]

Some blue-collar jobs are not going to be enhanced by technology. The right environment, though, can make the difference for these workers. An intelligent, but uneducated, woman who has worked for a maintenance company for 14 years receives decent pay and benefits. Why does she stay in this "dead-end" job? She answers this question by saying how much she loves her job. Further probing revealed that she is treated with respect and dignity. The company supports her situation as a single mother of three children. Finally, the company praises her work and tells her how much it values her. In this case, organizational capital is supporting this woman—along with hundreds of others who would otherwise feel disenfranchised.

## Matching the Right Person with the Right Position

One of the requisites for leaner, more efficient companies is to hire the right people for the right positions. This means that we need to look beyond skills and knowledge to the interpersonal skills that are necessary for effective job performance. It's relatively easy to determine if a person has the right skills, education, and even work-related experience to be hired into a particular position. It gets harder when we try to identify what really makes a difference for performance. Consider the following examples:

**❝** *We need to look beyond skills and knowledge to the interpersonal skills that are necessary for effective job performance.* **❞**

- Successful salespeople need different competencies depending on the type of product or service they sell. Technical sales, for example, may require a strong coaching or teaching competency, depending on who buys the product. Other sales positions demand a strong customer service orientation. Even if the salesperson is successful in the sales cycle through closing, lacking these skills affects the person's long-term performance.

- An intensive care nurse who pays attention to every detail about her patients may not have the competencies to manage a staff of nurses in the pediatric ward. She may be so obsessed with details of attending to patients that she is unable to grasp the quick nature of decision making associated with managing a large staff.

- The banker who evaluates the creditworthiness of a company may not be the best person to manage client relationships. In looking out for the bank's best interests, he may miss business development opportunities because he is more risk oriented and doesn't focus on marketing.

- An effective manager in an insurance company was promoted to an executive role. After a few months on the job, it is clear that although the executive is excellent at carrying out a mission (a traditional managerial focus), she lacks the visionary focus that effective leaders need.

- The general manager of a retail store who has demonstrated competency in administration and achieving goals has been promoted to regional manager with responsibility for seven other stores. He is experiencing difficulty in managing his time, as he tries to give each store the same individual attention that he gave when he was general manager.

- A new technical support representative for a software firm has an outstanding engineering background as well as a strong commitment to client servicing. She is eager to help, but she is a perfectionist. She often complicates her responses with unnecessary additional steps. Customers like her but are frustrated because she goes beyond the problem, sometimes creating new ones as a consequence.

- The project manager coordinating the relocation of an office was selected because of his superb organizational skills. As everything is about to converge for the actual move, five of the team members want to quit. They have been working 16-hour days with no recognition for their efforts. The project manager is surprised to hear about their distress because, after all, they are achieving their goal on time.

In all of these cases, the person's skills, experience, and education were not necessarily predictors of success. How they used their performance-based competencies—managerial, coaching, persuasiveness, motivating, interpersonal skills, and ability to achieve goals— took on greater importance.

## Assessing the Position

Fifty years ago, we would give office workers a typing test that measured the number of words typed per minute and number of mistakes made. People with the swiftest speed and highest accuracy were deemed to have potential to be good secretaries. Of course, nothing in a typing test tells anything about a person's ability to read another's writing, demeanor in answering a telephone, ability to meet deadlines, and ability to rank priorities. This is why we need to look beyond the hard skills.

# $W$ORKPLACE TREND

*A person's mastery of interpersonal skills is as important a determinant of successful workplace performance—if not more so—than hard skills.*

Many of the assessments on the market do not factor in the talent versus labor equation. New diagnostic instruments are taking into account competencies that knowledge-based workers need to have for success. Psychometric tests take into account aptitude and personality. Creativity and innovation, for example, are increasingly seen as performance prerequisites. Increasingly, psychometric tests will attempt to measure factors like creativity and capacity for innovation.

## Assessing Interpersonal Skills

Each job position ought to identify the interpersonal skills that are necessary for success. These are practical, commonsense attributes that make the difference in whether the job is being performed to its fullest. The following examples represent a sampling of interpersonal skills that may be applicable for your company.

**Initiative.** People who demonstrate initiative are those who can think and act without being driven. They do not rely on managers for motivation. In fact, they pride themselves on the fact that they seize the opportunity to begin new projects or brainstorm new ideas. These people can work well by themselves.

**Empathy.** Empathetic people have the ability to project themselves into another person's mind to understand how that person thinks or feels. Workers who deal with irate customers will be well served to develop this quality.

**Follow-through.** People who possess this competency are able to pick up the pieces of unfinished projects and make sure they are completed to their desired state. Think of a highly efficient administrative assistant who shadows her manager and takes care of all the details.

**Resiliency.** This quality shows up in people who have the ability to bounce back after setbacks. A highly resilient person can work well in an environment where there are a lot of ups and downs. She will inspire her coworkers to pick themselves up from a fall.

**Persuasiveness.** This is a necessary characteristic for people who need to influence, or to be convincing to other colleagues or to clients. Their strength comes from their ability to get across their point of view without appearing to be pushy.

**Adaptability.** People who possess this characteristic are able to change environments, projects, or managers relatively easily. They "roll with the punches" and adjust quickly to new situations so they can get on with their work.

People who master the necessary interpersonal skills for successful performance demonstrate a high level of emotional intelligence. Daniel Goleman's research in psychobiology and neuroscience reveals that the emotional part of the brain learns differently than the thinking part of the brain.[11] Many of these skills can be learned, and taking time to become proficient will pay off for your people as well as your company.

Firms that provide professional development for interpersonal skills or emotional intelligence are enhancing the value of their people by drawing out more of their talent and potential. By so doing, they are strengthening the collective human capital of the firm. It may seem like the "soft stuff," but it goes a long way toward profits.

*O*NE SIZE DOESN'T FIT ALL

*Professional Development of Interpersonal Skills*

*One of the benefits of employee development programs is that you can create a customized program for each employee that addresses each one's specific needs for personal development. Too many companies send all of their people through the same training without regard to who needs what. Send your people for professional development in the areas that will help them the most.*

Bill Bonnstetter, CEO of Target Training International, Ltd., is an expert on matching the right person with the right position. "One-size human asset doesn't fit all," says Bonnstetter.[12] He feels that our biggest issue is letting our individual bias influence the hiring and placement process. One company he worked with was looking to hire a new president and wanted the position evaluated from the perspective of four different areas of the United States. In three out of four cases, the number one–ranked competency was "presentation skills." The board said it would never have thought of this. It turned out that the most important role of the new president was to tell this company's story to the investment community.

**66** *One-size human asset doesn't fit all.* **99**

## Communication

One of the most essential areas of soft-skill development is communication. Every position has a requisite level of communication necessary for successful performance. Position descriptions, however, do not articulate these requirements effectively. Telling someone that a position requires "strong people skills" isn't enough. Does this mean negotiation skills? Interpersonal skills? Conversational skills? Good listening? Sensitivity to the needs of others? As you can see, we need to clarify these expressions.

It's fair to say that effective communication is important for people at all levels in the workplace. Often, it is the primary means of conveying what people do in their job. A brilliant financier or an engineering genius has to be as effective a communicator as someone who works in sales or business development. *How* each of them communicates, however, will differ.

Mortimer Adler's classic, *How to Speak, How to Listen,* delves into the essence of communication.[13] He divides communication into four key areas: reading, writing, speaking, and listening. In our formal educational system, reading gets the most attention, followed by writing. The attention to each of these subjects dwindles by the time children enter high school. Even more striking is the academic neglect of speaking and listening as important competencies. Virtually no schools require students to study speaking and listening. The result of this inattention is that even well-educated people enter the workforce with relatively little training in the basics of communication. It's no wonder there are so many communication challenges in the workplace.

Because communication, then, is a key ingredient of organizational capital, it is essential to understand which communication competencies are needed for effective job performance. It is as important for a CEO to get a message across to the board of directors or the media as it is for a customer service representative to satisfy a concerned customer's inquiry. It is worthwhile to look at the various positions within your organization and identify and rank the communication attributes that are necessary. Here are some elements to consider:

- What amount of time is spent speaking one-on-one with clients, coworkers, or vendors? Are these short or long periods of time?

- Does the position have "scripted" dialogue, or is the individual responsible for creating the language?

- Is the communication style informative or persuasive? Does the person in the job understand that distinction?

- How much time is spent making presentations or speeches in front of groups of people? Do the people making these presentations feel comfortable in this role?

- Is the communication time sensitive? Do others rely on the timely communication from a particular position?

- Does the position require extensive reading? How much comprehension is necessary? Does the reading require analysis or critical thinking?

- How much listening is involved in the position? Does the person listen on the phone or in person?

- What type of writing is necessary for the position? Is it technical writing? Interoffice memos? Business development letters?

- Does the position result in a lot of telephone tag, resulting in leaving a lot of voice mail messages? Are the voice mail messages succinct and clear?

- How much e-mail communication is required? Is e-mail written with attention to correct spelling and grammar and an appropriate tone?

In addition to these questions, you'll want to evaluate differences when communicating internally or externally to peers versus managers or subordinates. It is important to diagnose the baseline communication skills for each position. People who have the education, training, and experience can fail miserably if they lack appropriate communication dynamics.

Effective communicators are able to express their needs and wants with clarity. Talented people who are superb communicators are an invaluable asset to your company as they can *express* their talent well. You want to avoid the opposite—talented people who can't articulate things clearly. Those types of people cost your company. Think of your people who communicate well as money in the bank.

## Why and How to Understand Your Communication Style

People handle themselves differently based on the situation. Great communicators know how to adapt their own core communication style to those of others and thus make the connection between people more comfortable. Recipients of your communication feel that you understand them. And when we feel understood, we open the door to trust. We've heard the expression that people do business with those they like and trust; said another way, people shut the door on those they don't like and trust. This adage applies in the workplace as well. If you have a level of mutual confidence and trust with your coworkers, you'll work better together. Consider the following questions:[14]

- Do you take a direct, bold approach to problem solving, or do you prefer to gather and evaluate a lot of information first? Would your coworkers say that you come to conclusions too quickly or that you take forever to make a decision?

- Are you enthusiastic and friendly to everyone you meet, or are you more reserved and cautious when dealing with others? Would you be labeled as an optimist or a pessimist? Do you tend to trust or distrust people?

- Do you like to juggle a hundred different projects, or would you prefer going through your to-do list one item at a time?

Would others say that you show your emotions or that you have a great poker face?

- Do you have excellent attention to detail or do you wing it? Would people say that you follow the rules or break the rules? Do you comply with authority, or do you act independently?

Effective communicators know how to ramp up or turn down these and other variables. By "reading" your audience and adapting your communication style to theirs, you will enhance the effectiveness of your performance.

Effective communication is an important element for successful organizational capital. The ability to collaborate and communicate well across organizational lines is essential; and companies that place a high value on strong communication will be rewarded by higher workplace effectiveness.

## Final Thoughts

Organizations are dynamic, living systems and evolve through various changes that depend on human input. Today, your firm may have a more hierarchical structure but is striving for a more matrixed approach. Tomorrow, a market event may prompt you to revert to the hierarchical structure for the good of the company. The collective energy of an organization contributes to the effectiveness of its organizational capital.

Knowledge-based companies need to be committed to the ongoing training and education of their people. Organizational capital includes access to these opportunities. The discussion of communication brings to light how little we study an area that is often the critical success factor. It would be great if everyone in the workplace was self-motivated to go to classes and continue learning, but even the most enthusiastic workers are constrained by so many competing priorities that continuing education falls to a lower-level priority.

Companies should make training available for both hard and interpersonal skills. It is important to shift the corporate mind-set from training as a *cost* to training as an *investment*. When you think of human capital as the foundation of your company's value, you have no choice other than to take actions that will enhance the asset of human capital. Invest in your talent, and you will increase your organizational capital and overall value of your firm.

## CHAPTER RECAP

### Workplace Trends

- Value is now created at all levels within an organization, not just at the top layers.

- The Internet will increasingly be used as a vehicle for employee discussion and lobbying for benefits and compensation issues.

- A person's mastery of interpersonal skills is now considered as important a determinant of successful workplace performance—if not more so—than hard skills.

### Summary of Key Ideas

- Organizational capital provides the infrastructure and support that help to enhance the value of your people.

- The dismantling of hierarchies, combined with the shift in power from employers to workers, results in a more fragile workplace dynamic.

- When you give people the responsibility and authority to do their job, the results can be exceptional.

- Access to information has shattered the notion of senior manager as guru.

- Networked organizations typically have self-managing project teams that function autonomously.

- The "casualization" of the workplace has visually diffused lines of authority.

- Companies need to treat their people as talent to be nurtured rather than as labor to be taken for granted.

- Blue-collar workers can be retooled into knowledge workers if companies invest in training.

- Create a distinct value proposition for all employees to have a strong understanding of how their work contributes to the firm's results.

- We need to look beyond skills and knowledge to the "interpersonal skills" that are necessary for effective job performance.

- One-size human asset doesn't fit all.

- Understanding your communication style and adapting it to the style of others enhances job performance.

## Thinking Points

- Does your organizational capital provide sufficient infrastructure and support for your people?

- How effectively does your organization communicate across organizational lines?

- Does your firm have a central knowledge bank that is shared by all of your people? Is this something that your company would benefit from establishing?

- What is your company's policy regarding training and development for blue-collar workers?

- How would you evaluate your company's progress in the mastery of interpersonal skills?

## CHAPTER 7

# Employee Development

No one thought it could be done. But on May 6, 1954, British middle-distance runner Roger Bannister ran the mile in 3:59.4, breaking the four-minute barrier for the first time. Roger Bannister *believed* that he could run the mile in less than four minutes; his reality filter indicated he could, while the rest of the world couldn't see it. The impossible had been achieved, and running track hasn't been the same since.

On May 15, 1941, New York Yankee Joe DiMaggio hit a single off Eddie Smith of the Chicago White Sox and got at least a base hit in every game for the next 56 games, making his the hottest hitting streak in baseball that no one has touched since.

Today, Tiger Woods attracts worldwide attention and excitement to the game of golf. His mastery of the game and continual striving to achieve new performance records have received a lot of attention. A vision of what he wants to accomplish, endless hard work, and determination are among the characteristics that drive him to break new records. After winning the Masters for the first time in 1997, Woods left the tournament circuit for an unprecedented 18 months to perfect his swing. On returning to the competitive circuit, he broke through to seemingly unobtainable records. Tiger Woods holds a belief that he can win any tournament and a disbelief that he would lose one.

The world of sports provides us with new ways of looking at corporate performance. This isn't to suggest that workers start to train like elite athletes. Instead, stories of sports heroes inspire us to imagine *what is possible for achievement*. In recent years, sports psychologists have advised companies how their people can achieve peak performance. People are usually highly motivated after meeting with and/or listening to these consultants, whether in a one-on-one session or as an audience member during a motivational speech.

But how long does that inspiration last? What is done to reinforce the message and the learning that result from these sessions? The truth is that although others can inspire us, we are the only ones who can motivate ourselves. Internal motivators drive each person, and our work needs to fulfill the drive behind these motivators. Otherwise, millions of people will be in jobs that don't feed into their motivational core. They go through the motions and are essentially marking time until they no longer work in those jobs.

Sports superstars approach performance from a different perspective than do traditional corporate executives. Firms may have their people do some goal setting as part of performance management, but often this goal setting is task oriented rather than strategic. We can borrow a chapter from elite athletes who start with an enormous personal vision that drives the performance process. Once the vision is established, it is essential to have a strategy to achieve it. Is your firm doing this sort of employee-development work? If not, you're only scratching the surface of your people's potential. Employee-development strategies are one of the best ways to bring out the value of our firms' human capital.

In order to create effective employee-development programs, however, we need to first step aside and assess how our attitudes and beliefs affect our performance. Everyone has heard the adage, "You are what you think about." What you think about is one of the fundamental determinants of job performance. Understanding how it fits in helps us develop and execute effective employee-development programs.

## Personal Beliefs and Attitudes

Everything that we do or say reflects our underlying beliefs and attitudes. By understanding the relationship between them, we can better understand both what limits and what motivates us. Recognizing our limitations is the first step toward making substantive changes that affect performance.

## Beliefs

Beliefs represent our mental acceptance of something as true, conclusions we derive from information or experience. We can have a belief, for example, that a project is easy or difficult based on a prior experience with a similar project. Or we can derive beliefs based on what other people tell us. Beliefs are filters for reality. You see the world not as it is but *as you are.* Beliefs affect everything, from self-esteem to job performance, from relationships to prosperity. Our beliefs control our perceptions. And these perceptions become our attitudes.

Have you ever worked diligently to achieve a certain outcome, yet no matter how hard you tried, you didn't accomplish it quite to your satisfaction? You may have the skills and aptitude to achieve it, have a strong infrastructure and support network to accomplish it, but something is lacking. This missing element may be your underlying belief in the goal.

"You are what you think about" goes to the core of the importance of beliefs. Robert M. Williams, founder of the PER-K Centre for Exceptional Performance, offers this definition: "Beliefs are your perceptions of reality that have been created by conclusions derived from experience or information. Beliefs can be conscious or subconscious."[1] Williams recommends using techniques that can access and communicate directly with your subconscious mind. "The 20th century was the century of time management. The 21st century will be the century of mind management," Williams says. "The key is not just mind management that sets goals consciously and carries out the goals. You need to align your subconscious beliefs with your conscious goals."

## *W*ORKPLACE TREND

*The 21st century will be the century of mind management.*

For centuries, people believed that the earth was flat. That belief was challenged and eventually replaced with the new belief that the earth was round. A few centuries ago, doctors believed that the way to cure sick patients was to bleed them to rid the body of the ailment. That belief was challenged and patients were no longer bled. People didn't believe it was possible to run the mile in less than four minutes; once Roger Bannister broke the barrier, other top runners began to achieve this goal as well.

All of these are examples of how beliefs can affect outcomes. Our own beliefs may appear subtler than whether the earth is round or flat, but the impact on our performance can be just as monumental. Test yourself by honestly agreeing or disagreeing with the following statements:

- I am completely capable of doing my job.

- My performance reflects my abilities.

- I am confident about my performance in spite of what anyone else says.

- My thoughts affect my performance.

- My behavior reflects my attitudes.

If you answered no to any of these statements, it is clearly in your best interest to work on changing these self-limiting beliefs. When you imagine how your people are affected by limiting beliefs, you realize how powerfully this can affect performance.

Williams suggests that people who want to achieve exceptional performance should create an alignment between their conscious and subconscious goals. He tells us: "You can rewrite the software of your mind in order to change the printout of your performance." Changing self-limiting beliefs produces a chain reaction that transforms our thoughts, our words, and our actions. Here are some of the positive outcomes that can result from changing your self-limiting beliefs:

- You can become more effective on the job.

- Your effectiveness in working on a team improves.

- Your ability to convey your ideas is enhanced.

- You feel more aligned with your company mission and goals.

- You decide to make the changes that have been keeping you in a self-sabotaging environment.

No matter what your current situation is, it is empowering to know that you can change the outcome. Many of us plod along for years not realizing what the missing ingredient is. Skill-based training, inspirational books, affirmations, and motivational seminars are all worthy endeavors. Going to the core and changing self-limiting beliefs will reinforce all of this other hard work and take you the extra step to exceptional performance.

Using another sports analogy, think about a group of extremely gifted athletes who have had the same training, work out with the same amount of time and intensity, work with the same coach, and so on. Yet one of these talented individuals has the extra ingredient of a clear belief, consciously and subconsciously, that she is the champion.

## Motivating Attitudes

The attitudes that emerge from our thousands of beliefs are the foundation of what drives us, and understanding what drives us brings us another step closer to effective performance management. If someone works in a job that doesn't fulfill underlying needs, a constant struggle almost always ensues. Everyone has one or two key motivators. Knowing your drivers reinforces what you're doing in your current position or implies that you're not in a position to reach your potential.[2]

**The search for knowledge.** People who are motivated by a search for knowledge are constantly seeking to learn, as it is never too early or too late to learn something new. These people are interested in the "why" behind the everyday and the complex. They go through a thoughtful reasoning process and look at life objectively. Engineering and researching are examples of careers that make sense for these individuals.

**A balanced and harmonious environment.** This motivator implies a desire to exist in an environment that has unity and beauty. People who strive for such an environment have an interest in personal achievement and self-actualization. They view life subjectively and appreciate any form of creative expression. These people are motivated when they work in professions where their creative expression can be fulfilled.

**Power orientation.** People driven by power want to control their life and/or the life of others. They like being in charge and influential. Many CEOs and managers possess this attitude as do many politicians. A person driven by power needs to be in charge of something on the job.

**Helping others.** People who have an inherent love of others and want to make the world a better place are driven by the desire to help. They are selfless in their approach to others and are always the first to extend a helping hand. People who are driven by this attitude can be social workers or therapists or work in other "helping" professions.

**Productivity and economy.** Those who are driven by this attitude focus on efficiency, seeking a return on investment of time, talent, and resources. They may be driven by money but are driven more by productivity. They don't like to waste time or resources unnecessarily. Many business people, CEOs, and entrepreneurs are motivated by an interest in productivity and economy.

**Ideology.** Ideologically driven people are motivated by a way of life—their own "rule book." They have a set way of doing things, and those who work with them need to be aware of these rules so they don't inadvertently rock the boat. Appropriate careers are those that enhance these people's way of living.

When people understand the particular interest that drives them, they can easily see whether they are fulfilling that interest on the job. If not, they can still be effective if they are fulfilling their driving attitudes in some other aspect of their personal life.

It is also important to understand that your two primary drivers may inherently conflict with each other. For example, someone who is driven by economy and productivity ("I want to make money and take care of myself") may also be driven by helping others ("I want to make the world a better place—here's my money"). Curiously, both interests can be satisfied. The key is making sure that the person understands the distinctions and knows how to manage the conflict when competing interests "show up." Understanding the subtle dynamics of your employee's attitudes and interests makes a big difference in everything from job placement to determination to completing projects. Managers who comprehend these nuances are more effective in orchestrating positive outcomes from their people.

## Behavior

Our attitudes, then, influence our conduct. If someone has a power-oriented attitude, for example, he or she may act in a way that exudes confidence and authority. If our attitudes reflect what motivates us—*why* we do what we do—our behavior represents *how* we do what we do; and our communication style echoes our behavior. (Please refer to Chapter 6 to review these distinctions.)

## The Cycle of Beliefs

All of these components are linked. Our beliefs are conclusions we derive from information or experience. These beliefs affect our perceptions, which then form our attitudes. In turn, our attitudes affect our behavior. Our behavior reinforces our underlying beliefs. In a nutshell, your actions are based on your underlying beliefs. Let's look at a nonbusiness example to illustrate this point. As a child, you may have been traumatized when your next-door neighbor's large golden retriever overzealously barked at you when you were innocently standing in the yard holding a stick. Not knowing that Rover was waiting for you to throw the stick, you got scared and ran away. Rover followed, barking, still determined to get that stick. As you got older, other exuberant, barking dogs reinforced this fear. You devel-

**FIGURE 7.1**   The Cycle of Beliefs

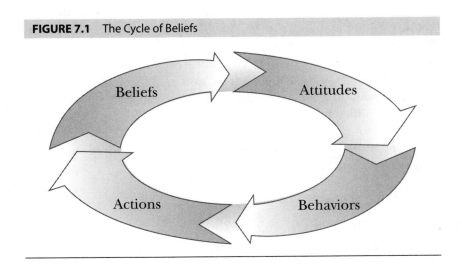

oped an attitude that big dogs were mean and should be avoided, which led to your avoiding contact with big dogs (behavior). One day, you were caught off guard by a barking retriever, reinforcing your attitude that big dogs should be avoided. The result reinforced your belief. As long as you continue to hold those underlying beliefs, behavioral changes will be difficult because the attitude and resultant behavior are derived from your beliefs.

The same thing happens on the job. If you believe that your work is boring, more often than not it will be boring. If you believe that you are making a worthwhile contribution to the firm, chances are you will make more of an effort to do good work. If you believe that you need to suffer through endless hours of hard work to get ahead, your wish will be granted. If you believe that if you work smarter you will get ahead more quickly, you will.

## Changing Beliefs

If you want to change an attitude or behavior, you have to change your underlying beliefs. The cycle of beliefs can be broken by changing an underlying belief—in the case of the dog, changing to "I like big dogs"—and reinforcing it through attitudes and behavior. If someone changes an underlying belief and supports it through appropriate attitudes and behavior, new results uphold the new belief.

People use many different techniques to change their beliefs, ranging from traditional psychotherapy to visualization, from affirmations to meditation, and so on. Most of these techniques approach change on the conscious level, but our beliefs reside on the subconscious level. We need to communicate with the subconscious to initiate change at the subconscious level.

Our ability to change self-limiting beliefs into self-empowering ones is a subtle, but important, value creation strategy. Some extremely talented people may have doubts deep down about their competency. By changing to more positive beliefs, people can boost their productivity or revenue.

*O*NE SIZE DOESN'T FIT ALL

### The Cycle of Beliefs

A person's beliefs can be very deep and personal. We may think we know everything about someone, while knowing nothing about their core *beliefs. Think about the person who exudes confidence but deep down is afraid to make a cold call. Alternatively, there is the shy, withdrawn person who is gifted at quelling customer fears. You can observe someone's behavior, but you can't observe his beliefs.*

## From Performance Management to Employee Development

Traditionally, performance management has simply been writing and reviewing a performance appraisal with employees on a periodic basis. Often, there is little feedback in-between appraisals, which can be dangerous for both the company and your people. If managers are too busy to provide ongoing feedback, people will tend to keep doing things the way they've always done them, even if it's inappropriate or less effective than alternative ways.

A better approach is to create an employee-development program. Think of this as an individualized strategic career development plan agreed on by the company and the employee. The length of time covered by the plan can vary and could be between one and three years in duration. The employee agrees to achieve certain levels of performance on a regular basis and meets with someone who acts as the process facilitator. Where appropriate, the person's performance can be benchmarked against others in similar positions. The person's direct manager can facilitate this process, or someone can do it outside the department, such as an internal or external executive coach.

### WORKPLACE TREND

*Employee-development strategies are among the best ways to bring out the value of your firm's human capital.*

By establishing a plan, the performance appraisal becomes more of a formality so there should be no surprises by the time appraisal time rolls around. In fact, a person's "off-track" behavior can usually be caught during the year. After the source of the problem is identified, the person can get back on track in achieving her goals. Employee-development plans are a way that companies can demonstrate appreciation for their people. The process itself can be extremely self-empowering, which ultimately builds the collective human capital of your company.

## Career Track

The employee-development process is holistic and ought to include a perspective on the person's longer-term career goals. Putting the current position in the context of the bigger career scenario provides a context for what might be accomplished within the current position. Position goals can be set within the framework of broader career goals. And from seeing the connection to longer-term career goals, the employee may have more incentive to do well. These goals and incentives, at the same time, benefit the firm by bringing the individual's goals into alignment with corporate goals.

By having insight about your employees' career goals, managers can more easily anticipate progression and succession within the organization. Understanding, acknowledging, and acting on what is important to your employees may mean a significant difference in attitude and performance. This represents an important shift in mindset, which is not to suggest that organizations return to paternalism but rather that your company will do well by doing well on behalf of your people.

## Measuring Performance

Measurement is critical to the success of the employee-development process. The employee and the manager agree on the measures, based, of course, on the nature of the job. For example, revenue-generating employees, such as salespeople, can be measured in different ways—for example, the number of business development calls they make weekly, the number of client conversions, or dollar amounts of sales made in a period.

Some firms track sales per employee as a way to measure productivity, but a number of companies use sales per employee as a predictor of Wall Street's response to the company. Because people account for such a large percentage of a company's operating expense, sales per employee is a measure worth watching. Some companies use the measure to monitor hiring, so that sales growth outpaces hiring. Others use the measure in combination with individual employee goals. By overlaying the two measures, some companies eliminate the bottom 5 to 10 percent of their workforce.[3]

You can also use measurements for non-revenue-generating staff. Here, the gauges tend to be productivity oriented. For example, the graphics department of a company might produce a certain amount of product in a month. If it is running behind, it has to outsource work. If the need to outsource work is because productivity has dropped, then outsourcing is an additional cost to the company; if it is because of increased demand, hiring more graphics staff may be indicated.

A number of companies rank the performance of their employees with the intent of letting the bottom 5 or 10 percent go annually. The objective is to continually raise the quality of their people in an objective, measured manner. General Electric is one of the companies that follows this practice. Jack Welch, former CEO, used to say that he spent about 50 percent of his time on people issues. He had a notebook that showed the ratings for the professionals in GE's various units. Using a rating scale of 1 to 5, the top 10 percent are ranked 1, the next 15 percent 2, the middle 50 percent 3, a questionable 15 percent ranked 4, and the bottom 10 percent as 5. Welch viewed the middle tier as the ones with the greatest potential.[4] Given the grade inflation that exists in our school system, it is interesting to think of the vast majority of GE's talent ranked as 3.

Other types of assessments can measure a person's performance by evaluating management style and other interpersonal skills. Especially popular have been 360° feedback tools. Please note that these will be more effective tools if they measure competencies that are relevant to the person being evaluated; many tools assess a random list of skills that may not be appropriate.

## Education and Training

Chapter 4 established that companies that invest in training and education benefit by increasing shareholder return. How then do you determine the appropriate training for your people? Following are some suggestions.

**Skills-based training.** Do your people need additional training in software or technology? Do they need specific sales training on how to become better prospectors or better closers? Do they need to obtain continuing education credits if they are lawyers, accountants, or other professionals whose professional licenses require ongoing education?

**Interpersonal skills training.** Identify the interpersonal skills that drive performance in particular positions to determine what will enhance corporate performance. The skills could range from presentation to negotiating to enhanced customer service to time management. As discussed in the last chapter, the broad array of interpersonal skills is often the area that makes the difference between adequate performance and strong performance in a particular position.

**Ongoing education.** Does your firm provide tuition reimbursement? This is perceived as a valuable benefit for your staff. By placing a high value on education, your firm will be aided in its efforts to attract and retain good people. Much of the emphasis on external education is in the area of executive education. The number of executive MBA programs has grown significantly in recent years, and many prestigious MBA programs are partnering with others in different parts of the world to give a global leadership perspective to its students.

**e-Learning.** The growth of the Internet has spawned many e-learning options. This has been an effective venue, particularly for companies that have geographically dispersed staff. It is also effective for workforces that work 24/7, as people can attend courses at their convenience. Cisco has used e-learning effectively. Its internal training department is responsible for training 4,000 salespeople, 15,000 partner organizations, and many more thousands of customers on new products. It created Field E-learning Connection (FELC), a Web site that aggregates information from the field and redistributes it to people who need to access it. One of its more attractive features is the democratization of its content creation, whereas its distribution is centralized.[5]

**Corporate universities.** A number of companies have established corporate universities as vehicles to provide enhanced education in such areas as marketing, technology, and business development. Over the decade of the 1990s, the number of these facilities grew from 400 to over 1,600 in the United States by the year 2000.[6] McDonald's Hamburger University is one of the more famous of these operations, having trained over 50,000 managers since its inception in 1963.[7]

Corporate universities provide on-site and Internet-based study, focusing on corporate core competencies. Larger companies also provide simultaneous translation for their workers from other countries. In addition to training a firm's employees, corporate universities are also used as training facilities for customers and suppliers.

## Sales

As salespeople are primarily responsible for generating revenue, it is particularly important to make sure that they have continuous cutting-edge training and development. William T. Brooks, CEO of the Brooks Group, a sales and sales management consulting firm, has repeatedly seen situations in which top salespeople leave their companies because of inadequate training and support. He observes that most companies make available only basic product-oriented training programs, while the salespeople are left to fend for themselves. "If it's really going to work, the sales training effort never stops," Brooks comments. "The most effective [companies] empower their sales management team to be in the field coaching, training, and reinforcing their salespeople." [8]

Training and education are important for people at all levels of your firm. It is worthwhile to identify and establish regular training goals for your people as part of your employee-development strategy. This supports lifelong learning goals and also sends a strong message that your firm wants to enhance the value of its people.

## Reengineering the Performance Appraisal

Some firms use the same performance appraisal for people at all levels of the company. A standardized form is not the best way to measure performance of talent. Most managers write appraisals annually, usually at the time that raises are being determined for the following year. Although this may be an administratively easy way to handle the task, it is a system filled with flaws. If you give someone an outstanding performance appraisal with a 5 percent salary increase at the same time that you give an average performer a 3 percent increase, you are sending out a message that excellent performance is worth only 2 percent more.

Employee-development programs are more proactive. You can work with your people to set short-term and long-term performance objectives as well as identify education and training goals. Ideally, the employee-development program is an ongoing process of review and discovery as opposed to an annual review tied to salary increases. By approaching your people's development continuously instead of statically, you can identify everything from course corrections to new opportunities. Employee-development programs enhance human capital while concurrently making people feel valued.

## Coaching

In some cases, coaching is appropriate for enhancing employee development. Some of the obvious opportunities to do this include promotions, job changes, and structural changes (such as a restructuring or merger), as well as times when performance is suffering on some level. Coaching can provide ongoing support to the employee with specific focus on the area of development.

A newly promoted manager may need help in developing or strengthening competencies necessary for the new position. A coach can assist this person in improving these attributes as well as being a sounding board for concerns that may arise during the transition of responsibilities. The coach may also act as an accountability partner. Accountability can be a great motivator; by having an objective partner in the process, the new manager can accomplish goals in a nonthreatening and supportive environment.

High-tech industries have bought into the idea of using coaches. As technical people collaborate more intimately with "lay people," it has raised the bar on the level of interpersonal skills necessary for good performance.[9] Coaching has been used as an employee retention tool in these companies. It has also helped cultivate customer relationships, as customers have become much more demanding and assertive since the emergence of the Internet.

Coaches are also used to working with employees who may have shortcomings in interpersonal skills. A senior financial executive, for example, has demonstrated competence in the hard skills necessary to do her job. She isn't reaching her potential, however, because her communication style offends her coworkers, who feel she is arrogant and go out of their way to avoid her. She isn't aware of her arrogant attitude and is defensive about it when approached by her manager. By working with an executive coach, she has become significantly more aware of her communication style and is improving rapport with her coworkers.

Many employees feel that their companies value them more when they're provided with a coach. They feel recognized and appreciated; seeing the results of working with a coach, they feel more self-empowered. The double benefit is obvious: the employee feels valued and the company gets enhanced performance. It is a win-win for both parties.

## Accelerated Performance

You may have a group of employees who clearly have superstar potential. These people will benefit from special attention. Think of them as you would the elite athletes mentioned earlier. Identifying extraordinary performance objectives and giving them the tools to achieve them could represent a huge opportunity for your firm. Accelerated performers are motivated by extraordinary success. If you provide the tools for them to achieve, they will stay as important members of your firm. If you don't acknowledge their potential, they will leave. Achievers want to work where they can flourish and be appreciated for their gifts. Remember that talent gravitates to other talent. Similarly, achievers are drawn to firms that recognize and embrace what they have to offer.

# Health-Related Performance Issues

Health-related issues are extremely important when it comes to understanding performance. We are in the midst of extraordinary medical discoveries at the beginning of the 21st century that will produce monumental differences in our quality of life. We now have cures for ailments that were previously not curable. Brain research, genetic engineering, bioengineering, and ongoing scientific research have resulted in the elimination of many diseases and improved the chances for longevity of many of the ill. Many cancers are now treatable; and cardiac patients have been able to live longer than anyone would have expected—even ten years ago.

At the same time, however, there is an increase in a number of diseases such as diabetes, asthma, and obesity, which are more insidious in many respects than cancer or heart disease. Mental and emotional disorders, such as stress, anxiety, and depression, are also increasing and have a tremendous negative impact on job performance.

*W*ORKPLACE TREND

*Stress, anxiety, and depression are increasing in the workplace and have a negative impact on workers' performance.*

## Depression

Depression is predicted to be the world's second most disabling disease by 2020. In the United States, it affects some 18 million people, or one in five over a lifetime.[10] A number of new antidepressants are being formulated, and many therapies are emerging as antidotes to depression. Unfortunately, many afflicted with depression don't respond to treatment; and depression also provokes other disabling diseases, such as heart disease and cancer.

Not all depression is diagnosed. Often, people just "work through it," not realizing or acknowledging there are remedies to offset the symptoms. Depression has a major impact on workplace performance because depressed workers simply cannot perform at the same level as those who are not depressed. Managers must pay attention to their employees' mental health as a way to gauge the impact on their firm.

## Stress

The word *stress* is a catchall phrase in some respects. Not a week goes by when you don't hear someone talking about how stressed he is about something in his life. Work appears to be a big stress trigger, but the bigger issue isn't work in isolation. It's the issue of competing priorities and not enough time to accomplish a normal week's activities, including work.

**Job uncertainty.** People have felt stressed in the corporate environment from the late 1980s, not knowing if their job would be a casualty of the latest organizational restructuring. When rumors are flying, it is normal for people to feel insecure about their future.

**Economic uncertainty.** The situation is compounded by economic uncertainty. With companies laying off people at the first sign of economic trouble, it's not surprising that economic uncertainty is another job-related stress trigger.

**Takeover uncertainty.** Workers who survive mergers and acquisitions face new stressful situations after the fact. Whether it is guilt for surviving the cuts or worries about working for new people in a new corporate culture, their level of uncertainty can skyrocket. If management does a lousy job of preparing the employees, it makes the situation worse.[11]

**Financial future.** The shift to defined contribution pensions, such as 401(k) plans, has made individuals responsible for their own financial future. Companies that offer a matching percentage often do so in company stock. If the company suffers a setback, your people will lose as the company portion of their pension plan may decline significantly in value. This scenario has become painfully visible with the Enron debacle.

**Managing competing priorities.** As people work longer hours and work-home boundaries are increasingly blurred, people worry about their ability to balance everything they need to do. In spite of phenomenal juggling talents, balancing competing priorities becomes a huge burden, especially for working parents. If your company is not family friendly in spirit (and not just in policy), the stress becomes greater. Employees worry they will lose their job if they focus on personal issues, but they also worry that their family will suffer if they focus on the job. This is clearly a losing proposition.

**Information overload.** The overwhelming amount of information that comes our way on a given day—memos, mail, e-mail, voice mail—becomes overwhelming, especially when other stress triggers are present. A Pitney Bowes survey found that employees at all levels handle an average of 204 messages a day.[12]

**Dealing with technology.** People can become stressed from dealing with technology. They suffer multiple challenges in this area —software incompatibility, servers going down, the need to learn a new application under time pressure, for example.

Stress can lead to a number of physical ailments and discomforts, including exhaustion, stomach disorders, backaches, and asthma. And it provokes mental disease such as anxiety and depression as well.[13] Stress depresses the immune system, moreover, causing greater susceptibility to viruses and infections. Of course, the antidote to a stressful situation is to create more balance in your life— and thus the cycle is perpetuated into a chronic situation.

We are fighting our biological clocks. Increasingly, our production of melatonin is affected by being exposed to more light at night;

and studies have revealed that a reduction in melatonin can result in estrogen-related deficiencies, such as breast cancer.[14] People get up earlier just to have some time for themselves. According to the Sleep Foundation, we have reduced our average sleep by 20 percent in the past 25 years.[15] Early risers have higher levels of the stress hormone cortisol than do people who sleep later. Over time, early risers had more aches and pains as a result of suppressed immune systems.[16]

Stress affects people of all ages. Young people are feeling stressed from the pressure of trying to have it all and not feeling successful. Sounding strangely like a midlife crisis, this has been dubbed a "quarterlife crisis." Symptoms include a lack of certainty, an inability to predict the future, and a sense of instability.[17]

Companies that turn their heads to these issues are completely missing the point. The corporate environment is a primary trigger for stressors. If companies want to have productive and healthy work-forces, the issue of stress triggers must be addressed on an ongoing basis. A healthy work environment contributes to the health of your people. A collectively more healthy group of employees results in stronger human capital.

## Scientific Advances That Improve Work Performance

Although we have an abundance of health-related issues that can negatively affect performance, there are also many scientific break-throughs that have positive implications for performance.

### Gene Therapies

Athletes will soon be relying on gene therapies to enhance performance. Using the same techniques that cure genetic diseases, gene therapies will soon be able to aid muscle development.[18] Extrapolating from this example, gene therapies can eventually be used to enhance brain performance. Consider the advances that are being made to mitigate—and eventually cure—neurological diseases, such as Alzheimer's and Parkinson's. The same principles can be applied to performance enhancement as well.

## Intelligence

IQ scores have risen substantially since the beginning of the 20th century; for example, 27 points in Britain since 1942 and 24 points in the United States since 1918. Recently, considerable discussion has focused on the relevance of the IQ test. Researchers claim that although heredity and the environment affect IQ scores, genes cause "people to seek out certain environments, certain life experiences."[19]

## Brain Machine Technologies

Brain wave technology is being used by people who have motor disabilities but have normal thinking capacity to communicate. Thought recognition is used to communicate from the brain onto a computer screen. These emerging brain machine technologies will make important contributions in coming years. One possible application is integrating signals from EEGs with muscle signals to help people with cognitive disabilities.[20]

# Managerial Challenges

Clearly, the role of management in knowledge-based companies has been transformed. Slimmer staffs and significantly fewer managers have resulted in a different managerial paradigm. The question ultimately becomes, How do we motivate our people to achieve the corporate goals and objectives when we are operating with significantly fewer resources?

As mentioned earlier, no one can motivate anyone else. People can motivate only themselves. We can provide the tools and environment to create strong performance, but ultimately the person, not the company, drives motivation. Executives and managers can inspire, but they cannot motivate, which is why the environment of the job takes on such significance. People like coming to work when they feel they are part of value creation.

The key managerial role in the knowledge-based company is to make sure that the organizational capital functions properly. The right infrastructure and support provide the foundation for workers to achieve top performance. The melding of organizational capital with employee-development strategies gives workers the foundation for solid performance and advancement.

## Attention as Currency in a 24/7 Environment

Information availability and overload combined with 24/7 time frames have created a new currency: attention. We have so many different priorities competing for our attention today that one of our great managerial challenges is managing attention.

## Self-Management

People can become effective self-managers if they know what they need to manage. As discussed previously, people often don't know how they are being measured or how their particular job contributes to the firm's overall results. Employee-development programs, including performance measurements, therefore, take on new importance.

66 *Talent can best serve itself by focusing on creating value in the firm.* 99

Talent can best serve itself by focusing on creating value in the firm. Talent needs to continually ask questions that reveal a proactive self-management approach to the job:

- How does my position add value to the firm today? Has this value contribution changed recently or is it likely to change in the future?

- How do my customers feel that I add value for them?

- What value do I provide my coworkers that adds value for them?

- What sort of measurements do I use to quantify how I create value?

- How does this position add to my portfolio of experiences?

- What type of additional training or education will further enhance my value?

- Will working with an executive coach bolster my value?

This group of questions is an excellent foundation for reviewing your people's progress. As you can see, effective self-management can be a vital part of employee-development strategy.

## Final Thoughts

We are exploring new territory when we speak about communicating with our subconscious mind to change self-limiting beliefs. Most change techniques until now have focused on using the conscious mind to influence the subconscious; you would need an enormous amount of repetition to make effective changes that way. Quantum psychology and brain dominance theory are teaching us how we can make the appropriate changes so we can reach our potential.

Employee-development programs are strategically important ways by which companies can facilitate the development of their people. Talent wants to develop and expand its horizons, and these programs are tools that can help talent achieve professional goals.

As we become more effective self-managers, we shift more performance-related responsibility to ourselves. Because talent is portable and will go where opportunities exist to build its portfolios, self-management helps considerably in the growth process. Managers who support employee-development plans will be rewarded by the kind of performance that can only be motivated from within.

## CHAPTER RECAP

### Workplace Trends

- The 21st century will be the century of mind management.

- Employee-development strategies are among the best ways to bring out the value of your firm's human capital.

- Stress, anxiety, and depression are increasing in the workplace and have a negative impact on workers' performance.

## Summary of Key Ideas

- Stories of elite athletes provide us with the inspiration to imagine what is possible for us to achieve.

- Everything we do or say reflects our underlying beliefs and attitudes.

- You can rewrite the software of your mind in order to change the printout of your performance.

- Working in a job that fulfills one of our key motivators will lead to stronger job performance.

- The cycle of beliefs reinforces itself through results. Replacing a self-limiting belief with a self-empowering one can break the cycle.

- The employee-development process is holistic and ought to include a perspective of the person's longer-term goals.

- Performance measurements cam be created for both revenue-generating and non-revenue-generating staff.

- Training and education are appropriate for people at all levels of your company.

- Coaching is appropriate for employee development, for example, when people undergo position changes or need help improving their interpersonal skills.

- Performance-related scientific breakthroughs may soon be used in the workplace.

- Talent can best serve itself by focusing on how it creates value in the firm.

## Thinking Points

- Are your people struggling with self-limiting beliefs that are preventing them from performing to their potential? Are they open to changing these beliefs?

- Do your people know which attitudes motivate them? Are they working in jobs where these motivators result in strong job performance?

- What is your firm's employee-development process? What would you want to change to improve the process?

- What type of performance measurements are you using with your people? How can these be improved?

- Is your talent focused on creating value? How can you facilitate this process?

## CHAPTER 8

# Virtual Capital: The Human-Technology Interface

"It's 15 minutes before your three o'clock appointment with John Walman, CEO of Infomatics," says your assistant, Jean. "Do you have the Infomatics file and proposal?" This is your third meeting with Walman, and you are presenting a proposal for a project that will be beneficial for both of your companies. Jean reminds you of the personal connections that you've discovered with Walman, including your college friend-turned-banker Lauren Massello, who has known Walman since graduate school.

You tell Jean that you can't find your prep notes, and within minutes a fresh copy is in your printer tray. "Is there anything else that you need?" asks Jean. All you need now is directions to Infomatics, which Jean also promptly prints for you. She wishes you good luck and looks forward to hearing the outcome of your meeting.

This sounds like a fairly typical dialogue between an executive and her assistant, but not typical is that Jean is your computer.

In the coming years, the combination of increased computerization, enhanced broadband, voice recognition software, and other technological innovations will make it completely possible for us to work side by side with machines that think and respond like people. Technology is increasingly cheaper and more easily accessible so that anyone can use it. We have only a glimpse of how technology will have an impact on us, yet we know the impact will be huge.

Several precepts set the stage for understanding the impact of technology. Moore's Law is one of these doctrines; Gordon Moore, founder of Intel, observed that the capacity of the microchip has doubled every 18 months; and concurrently, the price of this capacity is cut in half. By way of example, in the early 1980s, a personal computer cost around $6,000, for which you got a whopping 10 megabytes of storage and 640 kilobytes of memory (which was an upgrade from the standard 256 kilobytes!). At the end of 2001, you could buy a PC with 20 gigabytes of storage and 1 gigabyte of memory for about $1,000, and this PC has more computing ability than most people will ever use or need in a lifetime.

The reality is that the most powerful and most frequently used computers of the future will not be the ones that we see on our desks but the ones that we can't see. Microminiaturization and increased chip capacity make any number of technological applications possible. Our clothing, for example, may have embedded microchips that control the temperature. Lunch orders will be automated and take into account any of our dietary requirements. Our office computer will automatically contact our home as we leave the office and initiate anything from making dinner to setting the thermostat in the living room. Think of this as microminiaturization meeting the Jetsons.

> ❝ The most powerful and most frequently used computers of the future will not be the ones that we see on our desks but the ones that we can't see. ❞

Another principle is Metcalf's Law, named after Bob Metcalf, the inventor of Ethernet and the founder of 3Com. Metcalf's Law states that a network grows more powerful as more people connect to it. The speed or power of the computer isn't as important as how well the network connects people. The Internet is a prime example of Metcalf's Law, in that the Internet becomes more powerful as more people are connected to it. Your personal network of contacts also becomes more powerful as it grows in size.

There is also a principle that governs the increase in broadband, a network that allows more information to be downloaded faster. DSL and T-1 lines, for example, provide greater bandwidth than a 56k dial-up modem does. According to George Gilder, bandwidth doubles roughly every four months.[1] As companies demand greater bandwidth and wireless applications increase, this doubling fundamentally changes how we do business.

The principles just discussed provide context for this chapter. The more your firm is able to maximize the interface between your people and technology, the more efficient and productive it will be. The stronger this relationship is, moreover, the higher the value of your firm's human capital. It's an upward spiraling relationship: The stronger the convergence, the higher the value; the weaker the connection, the lower the value.

## $W$ORKPLACE TREND

*The more efficient and effective the human-technology interface, the higher the productivity of the firm.*

In many respects, technology has democratized business. Smaller companies that superbly and efficiently use technology can compete with larger companies that haven't yet figured out their optimal mix. A small company can have a state-of-the-art Web site and appear much larger than it actually is. The site enables this company to compete globally, something that wouldn't have been imaginable to all but the most visionary techies in the mid-1980s. Companies can even provide real-time chat with a virtual customer service representative created from the next generation of software.[2]

**66** *Technology has democratized business.* **99**

Larger firms need to make sure their information technology (IT) departments don't take on a life of their own when the technology isn't serving the business. This has been the case in a lot of industries. The banking industry, for example, uses sophisticated technology, but this technology is mostly internally driven. When it becomes more customer and business focused, it will serve the banking industry much more effectively. A specific example relies on the fact that people are creatures of habit. If you typically withdraw $200 from an ATM, perhaps in the future ATMs will greet you by name and ask if you want $200 today?

We'll look in this chapter at how we're adjusting to the impact of more technology in the workplace and how the growth of wireless technology is influencing workplace trends. Technology affects us both on and off the job, and we will see how technological enhancements will affect us inside and outside of the workplace. We'll consider implications of time compression in the context of technology. Sociological implications of access to technology will also be considered along with the future merging of human and machines. Most important, the more efficient and effective the human-technology interface, the greater the value of your human capital.

# Adapting to Technology, or Survival of the Most Equipped

Discussions about adapting to technology occur in every office around the world. What is important is knowing the ability to adapt to technology is a mind-set. Neither age nor occupation nor education drives this mind-set. People who understand what technology can do, retain it in their vision. For some, it's a learned activity; for others, second nature.

People don't have to become techies to effectively embrace technology, but people who don't take the time to learn some technological innovations and use them will eventually be left behind. There were fears in the early days of the Internet, for example, that it would replace libraries and librarians. Today, libraries are flourishing and librarians have used the tools of the Internet to make their jobs more effective and efficient.

**❝** *Getting comfortable with technology isn't a one-time static event. It is an ongoing process.* **❞**

Information technology has resulted in substantially higher productivity, driven by people's willingness to try something new. Firms need to recognize, though, that getting comfortable with technology isn't a one-time static event. It is an ongoing process. New hardware and software are constantly coming onstream, so it is important to stay reasonably up-to-speed with changes. You needn't feel obliged to install every new software upgrade, but you do need to take an intelligent look at what the upgrade provides and whether it will enhance the productivity of the people using it. If your company embraces technology, your people need to keep pace so that their value as human assets can best serve you. This doesn't mean they must become techies, simply savvy tech users.

## Adapting in the Office

Virtually all office and professional workers use technology on some level. Our telephone and fax systems are examples of technology; using a PC—even if only as a fancy typewriter—is another example. And so is the Internet, especially e-mail. Although the use of e-mail has proliferated globally in the private and public sectors, there remain many who resist it. They fear becoming slaves to e-mail—a reasonable apprehension—so instead of learning to manage the process, they avoid it. It makes no sense to become a slave to technology, but it does make sense to welcome it when it simplifies your life.

Research has shown that firms concurrently investing in computer technology *and* human capital benefit from advances in productivity.[3] If they invest in one versus the other, the gains aren't the same. It is the combination of human capital and information technology that causes the increase. Computerizing a firm doesn't mean adding PCs to every desk on the floor. It means working differently, both internally and externally with customers. One of the main ways that technology changes white-collar work is by reconfiguring tasks that were previously done "more intuitively, but more haphazardly."

**❝** *Firms that concurrently invest in both computer technology and human capital benefit from their advances in productivity.* **❞**

Off-the-shelf software is now available for virtually every application in the office. It can track accounts receivable and accounts payable and manage all of your banking functions. Contact management software can manage customer relationships and provide up-to-date information for salespeople. Even filing can be managed by software. If you can't keep up with your upgrades or if you travel frequently, you can take advantage of application service providers (ASPs), companies that make software available on a usage basis from the Internet. You can access your account from anywhere in the world so that you don't need to load software and constantly update your working files on every aspect of your business to your laptop.

Many companies make the mistake of adding technology to the workplace without providing adequate training. When you add a new computer system or a software upgrade, it's necessary to provide initial training and access to a help desk to deal with questions that arise after the initial training. Managers often presume that their IT department will be able to assist staff with their technology questions. This isn't necessarily an accurate assumption, particularly if the IT department is responsible for handling the firm's central computer system and networks.

Firms should make their decision to add technology based on whether the technology will generate more productivity and efficiency for the business. Adding the latest hardware or software just because it's the latest new thing doesn't make good business sense. Although this might make your company the "first on its block," it will result in a lot of unnecessary downtime to learn and adapt to new systems. The more efficient and effective the relationship between your people and technology, the greater the value of your firm's human capital. Will using the software be more time consuming or time enhancing for the people involved? You may need to test different programs to assess the impact; not all applications have an optimal outcome.

66 *Will using the software be more time consuming or time enhancing for the people involved?* 99

An example of software that hasn't worked well is salespeople's use of CRM salesforce automation software. Many firms have embraced CRM software as a great application to track information about their customers. People from all over the firm, however, want to add their two cents about what should be tracked, leading Bill Brooks, CEO of sales management and training consultancy of The Brooks Group, to observe that salespeople then end up being the data input and data-gathering team for every department in the company.[4] On the surface it seems reasonable, but it takes people away from their primary task, which is selling. It takes them directly out of their core competency into something that not only diminishes their potential but detracts from what they do best. This example is dramatic because it effectively *diminishes* human capital.

"Someone who went into sales because they liked interaction with people is becoming a data entry person," Brooks comments. "So you've got people who like computers who won't sell and those who sell who don't like computers, and your productivity is way down. Talk about wasting human capital!" A majority of companies that have purchased CRM software have been dissatisfied because it hasn't produced the results they were looking for. Perhaps if these companies shift the data entry function to another area of the company, the software will be more effectively used.

## The Good, the Bad, and the Ugly about E-Mail

E-mail is the most widely used technology application in business. It has supplanted a lot of telephone communication, in-person chitchat, and traditional written correspondence. E-mail has enabled us to communicate immediately on a global basis. At the flick of a mouse, people are able to send messages, documents, or photographs to anyone anywhere in the world who has an e-mail account. E-mail has been a great tool that makes efficient business transactions possible for effective e-mail managers. It can be a bonanza for people who want to work more effectively.

Although e-mail has emerged as a substitute for both written and voice communication, it doesn't possess the intonation of voice or the discipline of traditional written documents. People's behavior changes with e-mail. Before e-mail, people knew how to spell. Now these same people send e-mail messages that are even challenging to read phonetically. It is difficult to decipher tone. People who write short, terse messages, for example, may be interpreted as being abrupt. Other people become time obsessed, expecting instantaneous responses to their e-mails.

Research by a Harvard Business School professor reveals that people share less information in e-mail than in face-to-face conversation, enabling an easier tendency to lie. E-mail is likely to lead to an impasse in negotiation, as one party doesn't want to give in more than the other. Overall, it works better for people if they have already met face-to-face and have established personal rapport.[5]

Another unfortunate habit is people e-mailing coworkers who sit 100 feet away from them. In these cases, e-mail breaks down the more natural way that people communicate, that is, talking to each other. A number of companies have recognized the absurdity of this practice and have designated certain days of the week as off limits for unessential internal e-mail.

E-mail clutter is competing, too, with paper clutter as a time management challenge. Instead of downloading messages, reading them, either deleting or responding to them, and going on to another project, a bottleneck often occurs after people respond to messages. Do you keep e-mail messages? If so, how long do you keep them? How do you file them? People who naturally accumulate clutter may feel overwhelmed by the digital equivalent.

When e-mail is handled quickly and with no glitches, it gives you instant gratification and satisfaction on the job. When people get bogged down in it, however, it is a complete drag on productivity. Workers who master the discipline will be ahead of the game most of the time. Using e-mail as a metaphor for other technologies, the point is to learn how to best use it for *relevant* applications on the job.

If it is used effectively, the value of your human capital increases. Ineffective use can result in tremendous lost productivity.

## Technology in the Field

Sophisticated new technologies are being used in the field as well. Blue-collar workers on construction sites use wearable computers so they can keep their hands free while sending and receiving messages from the office or other central locations. In a pilot program for Bell Canada, for example, workers in the field were outfitted with devices ranging from a computer chip that kept their outerwear warm to digital cameras attached to their hard hats to miniature keyboards attached by velcro to their sleeves to cell phones connected to the company's intranet.[6] Although these gadgets may have seemed awkward at first, the increased productivity resulting from their use benefited both the company and the workers.

PC-powered glasses are another application being used in the field. They create augmented reality for the wearer, whereby the wearer sees the actual world as well as a larger overlay of visual information. The Global Positioning System (GPS) can be used to keep workers connected to a central computer; and ultimately, this technology will be used to merge the real world with virtual reality.[7] An architect could be on a construction sight, for example, and superimpose the virtual reality of the completed project over the reality of a skeletal steel frame being erected.

Another application that enhances the human factor comes from robotic technology. Robots are replacing people to do maintenance work in sewers. Instead of submerging themselves below ground, former "sewer rats" have become robot technicians, who are now responsible for maneuvering the robots to do the work they used to do. These technicians receive ongoing training to make them effective operators of this new technology.[8]

## Who Will Be the Next Luddites?

Curious as it may seem, blue-collar workers may turn out to be using a greater variety of technology applications and may be more receptive to technological change than white-collar workers. Although job specific for the workers who use them, these technology applications can be parlayed to other industries as well. Microminiaturization has also resulted in hundreds of applications in our homes and cars. Maintenance and repair people operate less as mechanics and more as technicians today because they need to understand how the technology works to make repairs. Our cars contain more microchips than virtually anything in the office. In our homes, kitchen appliances, home entertainment centers, and security systems are all powered by technology.

Meanwhile, back in the office, people at all levels—from executives to clerks—have to feel comfortable using the information technology that is appropriate for their position. This means that executives will become comfortable in the basics of e-mail, for example, while receptionists will become comfortable using sophisticated telecommunications systems. The more comfortable your people are using technology, the more productive your company will become. If your firm has key people who are technophobic, you must decide whether to retrain them so they become comfortable or suggest an alternative job path. The *value of your human capital will decrease even if one key person resists.* That person's opposition creates problems for coworkers, resulting in a decline in productivity.

> 66 *If your firm has key people who are technophobic, you must decide whether to retrain them so they become comfortable or suggest an alternative job path.* 99

No matter where the person works or what technology is being used, for now people will be more comfortable when they learn to "think like software" so they can do their own troubleshooting when necessary. Intuitive interfaces are still not the norm, and until this changes, people will become extremely frustrated when they can't get technology to function the way they think it should. They try repeatedly with only the same unsatisfying results. Shifting the mindset so you "think like software" creates a new type of reasoning that will be used repeatedly in the near future until technology begins to "think like humans."

## *O*NE SIZE DOESN'T FIT ALL

### Technology Choices

*Too many tech choices are available for nontech people to decipher. Firms that activate the "latest and greatest" application without under-*

*standing user needs constantly frustrate their people. Instead, take user
surveys to determine needs and then choose accordingly. Make sure your
tech people speak your language.*

## Wireless Technology

Since the late 1990s, considerable discussion has focused on how
wireless technologies would change our life. Cell phones, pagers,
wireless personal digital assistants (PDAs), and wireless laptops hold
great hopes for the future. Technologies have combined, so now you
can buy a phone that is also a pager and a PDA and connects to the
Internet as well. The quandary is that the underlying infrastructure
for wireless technology hasn't yet matched the imagination of hardware providers. A simple example is the fact that we still have trouble
connecting on cell phones. Bad signals and dropped calls remain the
norm, not the exception, in many locations.

Wireless Internet access is consequently in a similarly primitive
state but will be an increasingly important technology in the future.
Wireless Internet access makes it possible for us to do business anywhere and still be connected to our firm's central computer or our
own desktop PC. There is currently no global standard, and thus dif-
fering levels of wireless quality are available to workers around the
world.

66 *Wireless Internet access makes it possible for us to do business
anywhere and still be connected to our firm's central computer or our own
desktop PC.* 99

Experts predicted that by the end of 1999 Wireless Application
Protocol (WAP) was going to be "killer app" for wireless communication. Japan was becoming a leader in wireless Internet access through
its telecommunications company, NTT DoCoMo. This technology allowed a constant connection to the Internet through cell phones. Not
only were the Japanese using cell phones for voice communication,
but they were accessing the Internet for everything from checking
news headlines to the stock market, horoscopes, and games.[9]

Scandinavians pioneered the electronic wallet concept, whereby
you can dial a number on your wireless device (your cell phone) to
pay for everything from vending machine snacks to gasoline. Mobile
commerce (m-commerce) allows Web-enabled cell phones to com-

municate with vendors. Imagine walking down the street and being connected to your favorite restaurant, which displays its menu and specials for the day.

Third-generation (3G) technology was predicted to be the universal solution for wireless by the middle of 2000. This technology uses a much broader bandwidth, which allows a cell phone to receive not just voice and text but video and images as well. The initial excitement over 3G technology has abated while infrastructure is built to support it. In the meantime, Americans, Europeans, and Japanese each operate on a different application, so the cell phone you use in the United States doesn't work in Italy.

At the beginning of 2001, European operators had committed more than £120 billion ($174 billion) on their 3G licenses and saw their share prices and credit ratings slide as a result of this investment. Faced with spending significantly more money on infrastructure, sales, and marketing, there is increasing speculation that commercial 3G services may be delayed even longer.[10]

In spite of the obstacles, wireless technology is dramatically changing the way we live and work. PDAs are being used by contractors in the field who check the progress of work as well as doctors who can tap into their patients' histories. Salespeople can access their home office's central database to find information for on-site client servicing in the field. You can be in the middle of a meeting and e-mail your office for a document that is sent to you immediately. Wireless technology will eliminate a lot of remaining lag times in business.

One of the challenges is that the technology may be more efficient than the people operating it, and this is why it continues to be important for those using the technology to understand the breadth of applications and the repercussions from using different applications. Wireless can be a tremendous productivity enabler—as long as the people using it are not bogged down by problems. When people are comfortable using new technologies, improved efficiency will be dramatic. The human capital strategy of wireless technology is a win-win situation if people embrace, and are eager to use, it to make their lives simpler and more efficient.

## Personal Implications of Technology

Because technology affects us in all aspects of our life, it isn't only a workplace topic. Microminiaturization, for example, already has resulted in tremendous home-based applications, such as the smart kitchen with its wireless control center that operates numerous microchip-based applications. The smart refrigerator, for example, knows when it's time to reorder orange juice based on your consumption habits; it automatically connects to an Internet grocer that will deliver your orange juice to your door before you even remember that you need to buy more. The fact that you *live* with technology enhancers automatically shifts your expectations of what is possible in the workplace.

## Families

Working parents use wireless technology to communicate with their children. As mentioned in an earlier chapter, many children carry pagers and cell phones as a way to stay connected to their parents. Kids can check in after school before going to soccer practice and call again to tell their parents they are on the way home. This has been a lifesaver, in particular for single parents who are juggling many different responsibilities between work and home. It helps them concentrate more productively on the job because they know they are a mere phone call away from their children.

Tamara Hareven, a professor of family studies and history at the University of Delaware, commented that she hasn't seen any precedents for the type of supervision that parents get through cell phones and pagers since chaperones accompanied young people on dates a century ago.[11] Of course, this technology also works well to keep families in touch when one family member is traveling. Dialing into a cell phone obviates the need to keep detailed itineraries on hand.

## Personal Enablers

At some point soon, microchip implants will be able to replace everything from your credit cards to keys. These chips will also communicate with computers in smart buildings, for example, automatically identifying you when you enter your office building. This type of embedded computing obviously has many implications for security while, at the same time, raising issues about personal privacy as it provides new alternatives for companies concerned about security. As companies evaluate their security options, they will need to keep in mind privacy issues.

Embedded computing also has medical applications. It can be used to release medication on a predetermined basis and monitor patients' vital functions. Eventually, people with medical ailments will no longer require repeated visits to the doctor, as their conditions can be monitored remotely. There are also performance enhancement applications for embedded computing; you could have a chip embedded in your brain to help with memory recall, for example. When personal enablers make sense, they enhance the productivity of the people who use them and therefore their human capital value.

## Digital Time

The merging of wireless and microchip technologies has resulted in new time-related pressures. Armed with cell phones and laptops, people are on call 24/7, with significant downsides accompanying this scenario. Attention is an important currency in the new economy, and certainly time is a key component of attention. Companies that want to maximize the value of their people need to stay attuned to how their people manage their time, including everything from product or service delivery to individual time commitment on the job. Velocity is driving businesses, and competition is increasingly between those who are fast and those who are slow.[12] Consider the following:

- What is the minimum and the maximum amount of time required to create our product or service?

- Are our customers operating at digital speed, and how does this affect us?

- What is our optimal response time with our customers?

- How does this response time change when we deal with customers on the Internet?

- What kind of time commitment do we expect of our people?

- To what degree is it appropriate to breach the boundaries of our people's personal time?

- How should our people manage the balance between personal time and work time?

# Workplace trend

*Managing velocity has replaced time management as a workplace priority.*

As introduced in Chapter 1, time is a knowledge worker's inventory. When time is used up, the person essentially cannot continue to produce. How companies monitor this scarce resource is an important human capital strategy. In addition, they need to make sure that their workers don't get burned out from overextending themselves on the job. Maximizing time enhances the value of knowledge workers tremendously.

**❝** *The merging of wireless and microchip technologies has resulted in new time-related pressures.* **❞**

Effective communication is essential in the workplace. When communication channels bog down, they immediately slow down whatever workers are doing. Think about the amount of downtime your firm experiences if a false rumor is hatched or inadequate information is given about an important initiative. Firms need to emphasize optimal communication as part of the corporate culture for effective performance. The elimination of bureaucratic practices, such as redundant meetings or administrative paperwork, is another factor that contributes to effectively maximizing time. Certainly, wireless technology —when it works—contributes to optimizing communication.

Companies can use the value of time to their advantage. Because time is so valuable, it has risen to the top of the list of luxuries that people want. Firms that offer time-enhancing comforts are viewed as understanding of the pressures of their people. Such offerings as convenience or concierge services, childcare availability, and on-site personal amenities are the types of amenities that people value today. And when people feel valued, they will stay late, come in early—whatever it takes to get the job done.

Your company's attitude toward time spent on the job is another area of importance. Is a 90-hour on-site workweek the norm, or do you encourage a 40-hour workweek for your people? Your company's attitude toward work time is driven by your internal culture as opposed to something stated in an employee manual. By encouraging your people to work less time, your firm will most likely benefit from a noticeable increase in productivity. In some cases you may notice a drop in absenteeism along with productivity increases if you restrict work hours.[13]

> 66 By encouraging your people to work less time, your firm will most likely benefit from a noticeable increase in productivity. 99

It's true that the Internet economy, with its 24/7 culture, has motivated a lot of pressure, but people have been working long hours before now. People feel pressured to perform and worry they won't have a job if they don't put in the hours. Competitive pressures have accelerated, and managers are demanding more of their workers, to which the blurring of boundaries between work and home has contributed significantly. If you can't finish your work in the office, you log on to e-mail after your children go to bed and work another two or three hours.

Companies that take the initiative to reduce the compulsion to work will reap the benefits. Aside from a significantly less stressed out workforce, an improved environment for creativity and innovation will be apparent. People can't be creative consistently when they are overtired. If your firm is perceived as being "time friendly," it will also be an attraction for talent. By showing respect for your people's time, you are saying that you value their time. And this is a big factor in overall value creation.

## Implications of Technology and Ignorance

Whereas we've heard a lot of discussion about the growing inequality between the "haves" and "have nots" since the birth of the digital age, a different issue for organizations to consider is the growing gap between those who can and those who cannot. "Cannots" are characterized by their ignorance about technology-related skills necessary to get ahead, but if they are not taught these skills, they will be left behind. Cannots can be uneducated or educated people—what distinguishes them is their discomfort with technology. When your workers don't expand their knowledge base, they put themselves at risk of becoming cannots. This is a tragedy, as bright, accomplished people can disappear from the firm's radar screen when they are perceived as nonfunctional in the digital age.

Your company can take the lead by creating the environment for the cannots to become cans—driven by corporate values and coming from the top. Creating such an environment means a significant cultural shift for many organizations. You can set up training for the cannots and also offer it to your customers' and vendors' staff, who may be in the same predicament. This strategy does not tie directly to the bottom line, but it makes a statement that you want to give good people the chance they deserve, even if they previously didn't have adequate exposure to technology.

Instituting a training strategy bodes well for your reputation as well as for the growth of your people. Your least technologically savvy people may be your most senior managers, not entry-level workers. Giving managers the tools to enable the better use of technology—and therefore more productive use of their resources—ultimately benefits your firm.

Over time, your people's comfort with technology won't be a competitive advantage; instead it will be expected. Firms that embrace technology early—and help their people to climb the necessary learning curve—will benefit by having a higher value of human capital.

**❝** *Your company can take the lead by creating the environment for the cannots to become cans.* **❞**

## Human-Machine Interface

The cybernetic future has arrived. We are approaching a time when people are becoming more machinelike and machines are becoming more humanlike. Many scientists and researchers agree that our future lies in the human-computer collaboration. New supercomputers are being developed that mimic the human brain. Large-scale biocomputers have been developed that are capable of real-time image processing, speech recognition, and logical inference. People, on the other hand, are becoming bionic—that is, their normal biological ability is enhanced by electronic devices. Someone who has a pacemaker for his heart, cochlear implants for his hearing, and a steel plate in his knee to repair a running injury is part man, part machine. As we live longer, this will become more common.

*W*ORKPLACE TREND

*People are becoming more machinelike and machines are becoming more humanlike. Our future lies in the human-computer collaboration.*

Scientist and writer Jaron Lanier has commented that, individually and together, medical science, neuroscience, computer science, genetics, and biology are on the verge of abandoning the human plane altogether. He observes that two technologies are challenging what it might mean to be human: (1) Biotechnology allows genetic manipulation through in vitro reproductive techniques; and (2) the merging of information technology and artificial intelligence may be leading to a new life form.[14]

Inventor and author Ray Kurzweil has extrapolated a future connection between the human brain and computers. The human brain's 100 billion neurons with 1,000 different connections result in 100 trillion connections that are capable of simultaneous calculation. The brain's weakness is in its neural circuitry; it produces "only" 200 calculations per second. He postulates that by the year 2020 a personal computer will be capable of about 20 million billion neural connection calculations per second, roughly the equivalent of the human brain.[15]

Kurzweil foresees brain mapping as the next significant undertaking, as huge an endeavor as was mapping the human genome. By using a brain scan as a template, we will be able to design neural nets that operate like the human brain. At some point, we will be able to download the contents of our brain and re-create it as on a neural computer.[16]

Computers are being designed to solve problems that programmers never envisioned during their design process. A computer program called a neural network taught itself how to play checkers without help from programmers. The program quickly defeated over 20 players in timed matches, raising questions about how far an adaptive algorithm can go.[17]

An offshoot of artificial intelligence is what some engineers call "evolutionary computation," which represents a group of biologically motivated ways to create new products and better-functioning factories and business processes. These engineers predict that intelligent agents will eventually be inside every piece of factory equipment.[18] Jaron Lanier is also discussing the possibilities behind tele-immersion, a technology that "approximates the illusion that a user is in the same physical space as other people," when in fact there could be thousands of miles distance between the parties.[19] This technology depicts people as "moving sculptures" from several different perspectives so that those present interact with images of people who are virtually present.

As companies begin to engage machines that are humanlike—we'll call them smart machines—a host of interesting implications for human capital emerge. For example:

- Who will be responsible when calamitous mistakes are made by these smart machines? Consider the possibility of one of these intelligent machines causing a disaster in your mainframe or on an off-site construction project.

- What sorts of rights will smart machines be given? Will they be the same as the ones we give to people?

- What benefits will these machines require and how will human capital policies and strategies affect them?

- Will smart machines be compatible with each other and with humans? Think about software incompatibility today, and then imagine what happens when smart machines enter the picture along with incompatible humans.

- How will we manage smart machines?

These points may seem amusing—and far out. But they represent the issues that we may have to consider when evaluating our human capital strategies in the future. People will presumably be the central focus, but it may be that the smart machines become the best enablers of people. The idea seems fantastic, but it's not a bad idea to stretch our thinking to consider the outlandish that may give us a glimpse of what could lie ahead.

We may conclude from all of this that we need genetic engineering more than ever—as a way to stay ahead of machines. Biotechnology may prevent humans from becoming an endangered species.

## Final Thoughts

Microminiaturization, the advanced power of networks and greater bandwidth, are influencing how we work. It's possible to envision a virtual workforce that operates on-site with clients rather than on-site in the office. The ability to connect to the head office by cell phone, pager, or wireless laptop changes the way we do business. Look at the example of the blue-collar workers in the field—people who are the future of the future.

Managing a remote workforce presents a number of challenges, not the least of which is maintaining connectivity among the workers. While virtual workforces will become increasingly common in the coming years, companies need to give their people the opportunity to physically be together. Virtual does not replace physical in the long term. Coming together gives people the opportunity to share corporate culture and reinforce their relationships with others.

Finally, it is important that companies pay attention to the can-cannot issue, particularly important if your firm has technophobic people who resist using technology. If they are left behind, they will rapidly become cannots, and this will eventually have a negative impact on your company's productivity. Taking this a step further, opportunities exist for firms to reach out into the community to help "teach the teachers" and thereby ensure that the coming generation in your community doesn't get trapped as cannots.

## CHAPTER RECAP

### Workplace Trends

- The more efficient and effective the human-technology interface, the higher the productivity of the firm.

- Managing velocity has replaced time management as a workplace priority.

- People are becoming more machinelike and machines are becoming more humanlike. Our future lies in the human-computer collaboration.

### Summary of Key Ideas

- The most important computing in the 21st century won't come from the computers we see on our desks but from the ones we can't see.

- Microchip capacity, the power of networks, and increasing bandwidth are the three key principles that affect how firms use technology.

- Technology has democratized business, as smaller firms have the capacity of doing the same things as larger companies.

- Getting comfortable with technology is not a one-time static event. It's an ongoing process.

- Firms that concurrently invest in computer technology and human capital will benefit from greater advances in productivity.

- Companies need to provide adequate technology training and support for their employees.

- Firms need to assess whether new technology will be more *time consuming* or *time enhancing* for the people using it.

- People's behavior changes when they use e-mail. E-mail overload can decrease productivity in the office.

- Wireless Internet access makes it possible for us to do business anywhere and still be connected to our company's head office.

- The merging of wireless and microchip technologies has resulted in new time-related pressures.

- By encouraging your people to work fewer hours, your firm will benefit by noticing an increase in productivity.

## Thinking Points

- How proactively does your firm adopt new technology and software upgrades? Does the pace of change fit the firm's needs?

- What are your company's e-mail policies? Does e-mail enhance or detract from performance?

- How is your firm using wireless technology? What is your "wish list" in anticipation of wireless infrastructure improvements?

- How is your company handling issues of digital time? Are your people managing the velocity of time?

- What is your firm doing to turn cannots into cans?

## CHAPTER 9

# Developing Leadership Capital

*Wanted:* Intelligent, charismatic, results-oriented CEO who can turn around midsized service company in three months under the direct surveillance of the board of directors. Reply to recruiter@sinkingfast.com.

This is the leadership challenge we face at the beginning of the 21st century. CEOs are in great demand and are being asked to accomplish small miracles in short periods. Boards of directors are impatient and clamoring for results. Publicly held companies are slaves to Wall Street, needing to produce results that are completely in line with analysts' expectations.

CEOs and other leaders are not given a lot of time to produce results. Under the microscope from their first day, they are expected to act quickly and decisively for the benefit of the company. Because it's unlikely leaders can accelerate sales in a short period, they slash expenses to produce a better bottom line. And slashing expenses in today's firms means cutting people. People represent a proportionately large expense from an accounting perspective, and the impact on a firm's financial statements is immediate.

Leaders are those who are accountable for developing the strategic initiatives of an organization and ensuring their successful outcomes. Leaders are responsible for gathering the best resources, including hiring the right people to manage and execute their strategies. In this respect, leadership is driven by a certain mind-set. People can have executive titles, but if their responsibilities are managerial rather than strategic, they are not acting in a leadership capacity.

So who wants to be a leader? Fortunately, many people jump at the chance. Those who work at companies that groom and build leaders, such as General Electric (GE), receive firsthand operational experience and leadership development. On completing this informal rite of passage, they are ready to hit the ground running. For example, when Jack Welch announced his retirement as CEO of GE, it was public knowledge that there were three potential successor candidates. After it was announced that Jeff Immelt would become CEO, the other CEO contenders were snapped up. Bob Nardelli, former head of GE Power Systems, became CEO of Home Depot, and Jim McNerney, former head of GE Aircraft Engines, became the new CEO of 3M.

GE alumni run at least a dozen other major companies. The company has a global reputation for not just developing leaders through its Leadership Development Center but receiving firsthand experience running the myriad of GE businesses. Many of GE's divisions, in fact, are larger than most companies in the United States. Because GE has an indisputable record of revenue growth and shareholder appreciation, it's little wonder that so many of its leaders are tapped to run other companies.[1]

GE has been unique in its ability to grow leaders. CEOs have the responsibility to seek out leadership potential within their firm because a lack of planning for the next generation of leadership raises questions about long-term sustainability. Companies that establish leadership depth within their organization are creating a strong foundation for carrying out their strategic initiatives. This is an important point, because in today's globally competitive environment, there isn't time to ignore the future leadership of the firm.

## Managing Velocity

CEOs are under fire to perform today more than ever before. Managing velocity is a requisite leadership attribute in today's economy. Competing demands from boards of directors, Wall Street investment bankers, and analysts combined with meeting and exceeding customer expectations and developing a top-notch cadre of human capital—to name a few requirements—mandate the ability to manage rapid change.

The development of human capital takes on entirely new dimensions given this velocity. Companies can't afford to get it wrong when it comes to their people; hiring ineffectively costs them both money and time. If they don't hire talent, they won't have access to the ideas and innovations that bright people have the capability to create. If they don't have corporate cultures that welcome and embrace people as value creators for the firm, corporate growth will be impeded.

CEOs can't fulfill their mandate without the right people. CEOs are leaving companies faster than at any time in history. Given the rapid turnover, executive suites are taking on characteristics of outplacement offices. Expectations are huge. Boards have become intolerant and are unwilling to wait a few quarters for results. CEOs receive heat from their boards if their goals are too moderate, so they commit to optimistic results and then get bashed when their companies don't meet their goals.[2]

Furthermore, if a company's culture doesn't embrace the value of its human assets, the company will be restricted in what it will be able to accomplish in the long term. CEO accountability is tied to the bottom line more than ever. If CEOs don't embrace human capital management and development, they put themselves at a competitive disadvantage. Obviously, CEOs aren't expected to have all the answers. But they *are* expected to have the best people in place so they can optimize the value of their companies.

### WORKPLACE TREND

*CEOs are being required to manage velocity, given the unprecedented time pressure to produce specific, measurable results.*

Speed drives most decisions. CEOs who wait too long to take action may lose an opportunity to enthusiastic and technologically savvy competitors poised for the window of opportunity to open. The churn rate of CEOs is accelerating to the extent that those who can't cope with speed and uncertainty are doomed. One observer pointed out that even old-style, archetypal CEOs such as Lee Iacocca, former CEO of Chrysler, don't have what it takes to survive today's turbulence.[3]

**❝** *CEOs who wait too long to take action may lose an opportunity to enthusiastic and technologically savvy competitors poised for the window of opportunity to open.* **❞**

Big companies are getting bigger. The responsibilities that go along with this growth are daunting. CEOs are constantly under the microscope and responsible for carrying out visions when they don't necessarily feel comfortable with all of the elements. Technology supplies a good example of the discomfort factor. CEOs know that their companies are increasingly dependent on more sophisticated technology, but those who don't "get their arms around this" are destined for extinction.[4] They don't need to understand technology; they just need to envision the possibilities and hire the right people to carry out the vision.

Small and midsized firms have different challenges. They are often confronted with market pressures without the resources to compete against larger firms. On the other hand, privately held companies have more breathing room, as they don't have to deal with the constant Wall Street pressure. But just because they don't have this pressure doesn't mean that CEOs of privately held companies are slow to respond. On the contrary, they are often leaner, more efficiently structured businesses that can make decisions and changes without a significant amount of discourse. They understand managing velocity.

Smaller companies that enhance the value of their people can be better positioned in the market than can their larger competitors. They are increasingly able to attract and retain top-notch talent simply because they understand that talent seeks an environment where it can grow and develop. Small and midsized companies that effectively enhance their human capital have a serious competitive advantage in the market.

Christopher H. Browne is managing director of Tweedy, Browne Company, LLC, a leading investment management and mutual fund company that has a relatively small staff in spite of the size and complexity of the portfolios it manages. Browne not only knows every person who works in the firm, but what is more significant, he can identify how each person contributes value. Tweedy, Browne has successfully matched the right people with the right positions, and, equally important, people in each of these positions are able to identify how they contribute value to the firm.[5]

Browne thinks that firm leaders must communicate clearly throughout the firm the importance of human capital management. He feels, however, that it's much more difficult to communicate the message in larger companies. "It's much easier to achieve it in a small-scale company where you can have a sense of everybody who's there," he comments. "You can really set the cultural tone for how it operates." As discussed in Chapter 5, the impact of a company's culture is pervasive when it comes to valuing people. Firms that place an intrinsically high value on developing talent enjoy the ripple effect of developing talent throughout the company. It's second nature—even intuitive—for leaders of these firms to embed strategies for developing human capital in their corporate culture.

Corporate culture can enable CEOs to manage velocity. The stability factor of a strong corporate culture makes a difference when steering a company through tumultuous times. Sustaining a culture that embraces people and gives them the opportunity to do their best can actually be an antidote to velocity. It can offset the intensity of speed by creating stability through the culture.

**❝ Corporate culture can enable CEOs to manage velocity. ❞**

## Leadership Competencies

We've equated human capital with talent, where talent is the collective set of experiences, education, hard skills, and interpersonal skills of a firm's people. Leadership capital is based on the same ingredients but differs in the mix and requires a different level of wisdom and experience, which doesn't necessarily mean age. Michael Dell and Bill Gates are great examples of visionaries who were wise at a young age. Leaders can distinguish themselves through their interpersonal skills. Although hundreds of books are written about what makes a good leader, the following attributes are particularly important as they pertain to the development of human capital.

**Visionary.** Leaders see the future and are able to envision the big picture before others can. They are savvy about trends and what affects the environment of their company, both from a business and personal perspective. Sometimes people characterize this as seeing the possibilities before others even knew those possibilities existed. Visionary leaders know how people can make the difference in the success or failure of a firm's strategies.

**People-Oriented.** We all have communication skills that fall into two broad categories: people oriented and task oriented. Although leaders need to possess both attributes, a strong people orientation makes a big difference. People-oriented leaders are optimistic about their people and what they expect of them, holding them to high standards and rewarding them for jobs done well. They are willing to delegate and involve others in decisions that affect them. They are great human capital strategists, knowing the difference that people make to the bottom line. Their people like working for them.

**Superb decision-making skills.** Have you ever worked in a company where the leader had enormous difficulty making any decision? The ability to assess information and circumstances and come to conclusions within a reasonable period is an essential leadership trait. When leaders waffle, they lose momentum and eventually lose the attention and respect of their people. Most important, the decisions that leaders make should have positive consequences for their people; if outcomes are negative, leaders can lose their people forever.

**Communicating excellence.** Leaders need to know the best way to get their message across. Whether making presentations to their boards or Wall Street analysts, or having a one-on-one conversation with a secretary in the hall, their ability to communicate effectively is essential. Part of this ability to communicate is stylistic. Strong leaders can be charismatic, and this contributes to effective communication. They can also be optimistic and thus engender trust. Some of them are direct and to the point, while others are friendlier and more persuasive. There is room for individuality in communication style. Its effectiveness will be measured in part by how people follow through on their messages.

Leaders also need to know how to listen. This is an extremely important attribute, as people have to know they are being heard. One of the most frequent criticisms of leaders and managers is they don't listen.

**Idea supporting.** Strong leaders facilitate idea generation. They give their people the environment and opportunity to explore ideas that lead to innovations. They are comfortable taking risks with new ideas that are consistent with, and support, the company's values, mission, and core competencies. Leaders run into problems when they stray outside these areas and try to add on or build without regard to how the innovation fits within the firm.

**Focused.** Leaders stay focused on their goals and objectives so they can achieve results. They don't initiate actions without following through and ensuring that the actions have reached a conclusion.

Leaders don't rely on others to control their actions. They act independently and put in whatever time is needed to get the job done.

**Ability to cultivate future generations of leaders.** As previously mentioned, firms need to develop the next generation of leaders to ensure sustainability. Many people are uncomfortable leading and have to be encouraged and coached as future leaders. Of course, not everyone will be a leader. Effective leaders have the ability to inspire their people to take action and commit to the company's vision and mission. Leaders who are committed to human capital development do this as a matter of course.

**Intuitive.** Intuitive leaders have the potential to bring human capital development to new levels. They have an innate sense about the value of people and will do what they can to match the right people with the right situations. Intuitive leaders use this skill for the strategic development of the company as a whole as well as individuals.

**Self-leadership skills.** This set of skills centers on personal effectiveness and self-management. When these attributes have been mastered, the leader reflects a certain aura of energy and self-awareness that magnetizes others.

The following traits are a subset of self-leadership:

- *Self-confident.* Strong leaders believe in themselves and their capabilities, even when things aren't going well. It's easy to be self-assured when things are going right but much more difficult to transcend adversity and maintain certainty when things aren't going too well.

- *Resilient.* This is the attribute that allows people to bounce back after set-backs and move forward with unshaken confidence. Although leaders need this to survive during turbulence, it also sends an important message to the rest of their people.

- *Initiative.* Leaders need to take the first step, which is often uncharted territory. The drive and ambition that underlies initiative is one of the things that separates leaders from others.

- *Self-responsible.* Leaders admit when they've blown it and take the heat themselves. This doesn't mean they become sacrificial lambs for every mistake. Rather, they admit mistakes, learn from them, and move on.

- *Ability to overcome adversity.* Many obstacles bar the path of a leader. The ability to surmount these hurdles and impediments is an important element of self-leadership.

- *Respectfulness.* Strong leaders show respect to themselves and to others. They understand the importance of maintaining dignity and honoring the uniqueness of others.

- *Trustworthiness.* Trustworthy leaders inspire trust in others. They do what they mean and mean what they say. They hold this attribute as a high personal value.

The attributes just described provide a framework for understanding leadership capital. Obviously, some companies and industries may require other attributes, but these characteristics are central to effective leadership capital. Given the brutal time constraints under which leaders operate, those who master these traits will be better positioned to survive and thrive when issues become more complex. By developing these traits, they enhance their own human asset value as well as their leadership capital. Leaders who strive to achieve their potential raise the overall value of human capital in the firm.

*O*NE SIZE DOESN'T FIT ALL

### Selecting the Right Leadership Competencies

*Leaders need to cultivate their best competencies so they can more effectively serve their various stakeholders. They need to master traits for interacting with employees, shareholders, customers, and others. They need to establish a personal development program that is customized for their specific competency objectives.*

Many leaders work with executive coaches to fine-tune their personal effectiveness, just as top competitive athletes work with coaches. As Tom Peters points out, leaders are rarely the best performers; they are better at getting the most out of others, not doing it themselves.[6]

66 *Leaders need to cultivate their best competencies so they can more effectively serve their various stakeholders.* 99

## CEO Capital

A fair amount of attention has been given the idea of the "CEO as brand." We've had a history of notable and charismatic business leaders, but not until the late 1990s was this considered a branding strategy. Because brands are an important intangible asset, we can conclude that CEO brands form a type of leadership capital that we can label "CEO capital." A very elusive concept, it is more difficult to quantify than any of the other nonfinancial measures of human capital.

Many CEOs are surrounded by the CEO brand mystique. Everybody knows the brands embodied in people like Steve Jobs, Bill Gates, and Michael Dell. Herb Kelleher put fun into flying at Southwest Airlines. Charles Schwab is a world-renowned innovator in financial services. Richard Branson is synonymous with the Virgin brand, whether it's Virgin Airways or Virgin Megastores.

Kevin Roberts, CEO of Saatchi & Saatchi, says that brands are outmoded. What counts today are such concepts as "trustmarks," whereby people have a significantly more emotional connection to companies. The term *Trustmarks* goes beyond branding as we know it, embodying factors such as leadership, authenticity, and the human spirit in addition to traditional advertising and marketing. Roberts makes the distinction that trustmarks belong to the people (the consumers), not the company. "Lovemarks" go even further on this spectrum. Roberts says that to create a lovemark, you have to be passionately in love with your own business; if you don't, your employees and customers won't love it either.[7]

Both of these ideas directly tie into the concept of leadership capital. They place importance on the story behind the company. Stories are about what *people* accomplish, not about your factory's productivity last month. If you have a love affair with your business, you have to be authentic. If you love your business and your business is based on people, imagine how attractive your brand will be in the market.

An example of this is the Timberland Company, a long-established family business whose CEO is Jeffrey Swartz. Swartz's grandfather founded the business by selling boots he had made by hand. He personalized every sale and stood behind the quality of the products. Swartz feels that the challenge to professionalize the company is to restore that personal feeling. He comments that consumers want to know who you are and what you believe in. "My challenge is to marry the boots and the brand with a set of beliefs that has fueled my family's mission for three generations."[8] Timberland, then, can become a lovemark.

## Developing Human Capital Management

Leaders are accustomed to tracking traditional financial measures, such as sales growth, cash flow, profitability, earnings per share—whichever measures are meaningful to manage and monitor a company's operations. Much of their decision making revolves around achieving the desired results. Whatever the outcome, the important thing is to achieve the projected results and not disappoint any of the powers that be.

CEOs must endorse the establishment of human capital management practices and assign someone to be accountable for tracking and analyzing the information. The nonfinancial measures introduced in Chapter 4 are as important for leaders to use as are traditional financial measures. Nonfinancial measures are geared toward enhancing the value of the firm's intangible assets, in particular its human capital, which in turn, strengthens the value of the firm. Leaders who require their firms to track nonfinancial measures, such as those related to attracting and retaining people as well as measures for education and training and incentive-based compensation, will be rewarded by being able to evaluate the strengths and weaknesses of their firms' human capital policies.

**❝** *CEOs must endorse the establishment of human capital management practices.* **❞**

### Attracting and Retaining People

The cost of replacing an employee approximates one and one-half times his annual compensation and can be even more for managers and executives. This is obviously a huge expense if your company has a revolving door for employees. Chapter 5 introduced ways to track recruiting and retaining staff. With those ideas in mind, here is what your people should evaluate:

- Calculate the rate of turnover in your company. Identify whether this rate of turnover fluctuates seasonally or cyclically.

- Determine the cost of replacing staff. This includes hard costs such as agency or recruiting fees, one-time costs related to departing employees, signing bonuses, and the cost of additional compensation or benefits. There are also soft costs involved, such as the departing person's decline in productivity, the start-up time for the new person to get up to speed, training costs, and costs associated with "not knowing" things that include everything from corporate culture to customer nuances to informal internal networks.

- Identify where you have recruited your best people and create strategies to enhance these recruiting efforts.

- Identify goals and time frames for improving your statistics, such as $x$ percent reduction in turnover within 18 months. Make it measurable and specific.

**Education and training.** As described in Chapter 4, investments in training and education pay off in quantifiable ways ranging from higher share price to increased productivity. Review your training policies and evaluate the following:

- Identify where your training dollars are allocated in the company. Determine the best use of the training investment and whether training should be introduced to other areas of the company.

- Track hard costs, such as money spent on courses (internally and externally), the cost of trainers and materials, and travel expenses directly related to attending courses.

- Track changes in a financial measure, such as increased revenue, productivity, or profitability in relation to your training investment.

**Incentive-based compensation.** You want to measure this across departments, tracking the different types of compensation that you offer. We know companies that use pay-for-performance compensation have higher results than those that don't.

- Identify the categories of incentive compensation used by your company. These will include stock, stock options, profit sharing, and bonuses.

- Evaluate where you can extend these awards so that more people are eligible.

- Calculate the level of straight salary versus pay for performance at different levels of the company, not just executive and managerial levels.

- As in the prior example, track these measures against revenues, productivity, or profitability.

## The Impact on Leadership Capital

Because CEOs are accustomed to measuring financial information, tracking nonfinancial information, such as the data mentioned above, is still new territory for many companies. Measuring things that have been previously unmeasurable is subject to bias and opinion, but it is better to create a system that can be tracked over time than to guess critical information related to intangibles. It is a key strategic decision to measure and analyze this information.

It is understandable that some of these softer costs are very subjective and difficult to measure. That doesn't matter. *What is important is to create a system of measurement that can capture, record, and track data.* Eventually you will have enough data to analyze, and you can then make more intelligent decisions based on quantifiable gauges.

It is important for executives and managers to have confidence in taking this course. Measuring nonfinancial information may cause consternation among some of your colleagues. You need to explain it to your board members. You need to assure your accountants that this information is *supplemental disclosure rather than financial reporting.*

Placing importance on tracking and analyzing nonfinancial measures is a corporate value, so leaders must exert influence over managers to make sure it is done. By starting to measure things that were previously not measured, you will know more about the company and that it is being better managed. The data are there—you just need to take the initiative to make it important. When you have enough data for meaningful analysis, you'll have new information that will help you understand the direct impact of investing in human capital strategies.

## $W$ORKPLACE TREND

*Visionary leaders are placing importance on creating a system of measurement for intangibles that can ultimately be used as a tool to enhance the value of the firm.*

Over time, tracking nonfinancial measures will greatly help you manage the firm's intangibles—in particular, its human capital. Understanding the role that human capital plays in your company and knowing certain specifics about its performance will help you and your colleagues become better leaders as well as managers of human capital. It will help your firm stay focused on its corporate core competencies. The people who work for you will feel more valued and committed to being an integral part of your organization. Moreover, you will establish a new degree of corporate clarity, something that will be reflected externally in your company's brand identity.

**66** *Placing importance on tracking and analyzing nonfinancial measures is a corporate value.* **99**

## Serving the Community

Most corporate leaders are active leaders outside their companies as well, serving on boards of nonprofit, civic, and community organizations. Because the association world is challenged by its shortage of professional staff and volunteers, business leaders who have mastered the art of human capital management can do a great service by bringing their expertise into the nonprofit world.

### Relationship Capital Building Community

Relationship capital can be a nonprofit organization's strongest asset, representing the collective relationships that are built among its members and how those members connect as a community. Associations are organized around a specific civic, community, trade, or professional interest, so members have a common interest from the start. The opportunity to build community, then, is one of the most powerful tools that a nonprofit organization possesses. And those that cultivate a sense of community are the ones that will be sustained and grow.

When associations build solid relationships among their members, they build a community. As that community grows more attractive, more people want to be a part of it because people want to feel they are part of a community. That is the foundation of relationship capital. You create a community that has a high barrier to exit from the beginning. People are more motivated to stay than to leave, and that naturally results in higher retention.

Although strong corporate cultures instill a sense of community, people find different aspects of this in nonprofits. Their primary reason for joining an association is its underlying mission. Going deeper, though, they want to feel part of something. Transferring some of your human capital strategies into the association world will reinforce this community building—the single most important thing an association can do to attract and retain members.

There can be a win-win exchange of value when corporate leaders contribute their time in the nonprofit world. They lend their expertise, such as strategic human capital management, and they receive a variety of benefits.

**Building networks.** Being a nonprofit leader is an excellent way to develop new relationships that can become part of your network. You will meet other leaders from other companies and industries and have a natural opportunity to broaden your network. Of course, networking is viral. As you expand your network through association leadership, you are also tapping into the networks of these other leaders.

**Creating lifetime advocates.** The same concept of lifetime advocacy that was discussed in Chapter 3 is applicable in the nonprofit world. In your association leadership role, you can build lifetime advocates from association members as well. You never know when these people will cross your path again and become prospective clients or employees.

**Associations as places of respite.** Associations can provide a respite from the time-intense insanity of the rest of a world where we barely have time to catch our breath. You can influence your organization to provide members with a place to breathe as opposed to a set of pressures that are comparable to the corporate side of their life.

Consider this: People in the workforce want to volunteer for good causes, work with good people, and feel fulfilled by what they do. Your ability to influence this type of environment will be beneficial to both the association staff and their volunteers.

Leaders of nonprofit boards can also influence how these organizations enhance the value of their members.

**Communication.** Clearly communicate your objectives. By taking the time to communicate, you are showing respect for your association colleagues. You are not putting them into the position of having to second-guess your objectives and motives. This is a simple concept, but doesn't necessarily happen consistently in volunteer organizations.

**Preventing burnout.** Allow people to make big contributions— but not so big that they start to burn out. One of the biggest challenges in volunteerism today relates to burned-out volunteers. Give members a chance to make a difference and have fun while they're doing it rather than creating stress around their volunteer work.

**Letting them shine.** Give your members the opportunity to showcase what they do best. People don't always have the opportunity to strut their best stuff in their job. Let your association open the door to developing their potential.

**Developing friendships.** Provide a forum for your members to tell their stories. Often, we connect with people but know only a small chronology of their work experience and a bit about their family. Telling our stories creates a level of intimacy that goes a long way in building relationship capital.

**Creating an alumni network.** As described in Chapter 5, alumni networks are vehicles to keep people connected to each other as well as remind them of their former affiliation with the company. The same principle applies in associations and has the potential to be even more powerful given the number of members and volunteers who revolve through nonprofits.

Corporate leaders who serve as nonprofit board members have the opportunity to give back to the community and influence human capital strategies as well as receive the benefits of an expanded network.

## Stewardship

Firms with a high level of leadership capital make contributions that help others who are less fortunate in the form of volunteerism or in-kind contributions. Many companies support the concept of their people working in the community; and increasingly, companies are encouraging their people do this on company time. For example, if your firm is committed to preventing the growth of cannots, as described in the last chapter, some of your people may volunteer in local schools or community colleges under the auspices of your firm.

Many law firms have historically supported the practice of allocating some of a firm's time to pro bono cases—that is, cases for which lawyers offer their services free of charge to those who can't afford to pay; in other words, to those who don't have access. Chapter 4 introduced the idea that we're owning less and leasing more, and it emphasized that access to goods and services is increasingly vital. The haves and the cans have access, but the have-nots and some of the cannots don't. Your company can leave a wonderful legacy by creating access to your products and services to those who otherwise would not have the right of way.

## *W*ORKPLACE TREND

*Companies that make their products and services accessible in the community are leaving a legacy of stewardship.*

Hewlett-Packard (HP) has pioneered a concept that some are calling B2-4B—business to four billion. HP calls this program World e-Inclusion, and its target market is the developing world. HP, along with its partners, is selling, leasing, or donating $1 billion in products and services to government agencies and nongovernmental organizations (NGOs) in places like Bangladesh and Singapore. It is significant that HP's program is not a philanthropy model. CEO Carly Fiorina comments: "There's a big difference between creating a sustainable business model around products and services that raise the standard of living, and aid or philanthropy money pouring in on an ongoing basis."[9]

Burned-out workers are being revived by taking leaves of absence when working for nonprofits. Companies such as Accenture, McKinsey, Shell, British Telecom, and American Express established partnerships with the British Volunteer Service Organization to donate people to work on projects in developing countries. These volunteers are making great strides in closing the have-not and cannot gaps.[10] And, as mentioned in Chapter 5, economic hardship has motivated other multinationals to offer people the option to work in nonprofits endorsed by their company as opposed to disengaging and working for another firm.

Indications are increasing that schools and school districts are recruiting heads of schools and superintendents from the private sector.[11] Because businesses can lend executives and managers as consultants to schools that want to operate more efficiently, they are likely to be significant partners of educational institutions in the coming years. Most schools still function on a manufacturing-era mentality—even an agrarian-era timetable when you consider the time off in the summer. Partnering with schools is another way that companies can demonstrate community involvement and leadership.

## Leadership and Value Creation

Firms that are driven by intangible assets must have leadership that is focused on their people. All of the innovations and creativity in the world are worthless if their producers do not feel valued. Simply put, companies that don't value their people will become extinct, and the initiative has to come from the top because it involves smashing old paradigms. No longer do you view your people as an expense; rather, you view them as talent to be valued and nurtured.

66 *Firms that are driven by intangible assets must have leadership that is focused on their people.* 99

People are the driving force of these firms, and CEOs who embrace enhancing the value of human capital will be rewarded by everything from greater productivity to less turnover to higher shareholder value. Human capital strategists underscore the need to have values, leadership, and corporate culture in place to effectively implement human capital goals. Measurement and analysis of human capital data are essential to increase a company's return on investment.

Chris Browne comments that leaders need to be curious about innovations and technology. "The person at the top of the organization has to be curious about innovative technology," Browne observes.[12] If leaders don't embrace technology, then, as Jack Welch has often said, they should quit and go someplace else, because otherwise they're going to be left in the dust. "Technology is not about kids playing Nintendo. It's a way to actually be more efficient," Browne says. "I can't program anything, but I can sit there and dream about what I'd like technology to be able to do and then get the people to do it."

Leaders who understand the linkage between technology and people will be ahead of their competition. Technology is an enabling tool that creates more efficiency within the company. People enhance the use of that technology and have the ability to create new ideas and innovations that create even more value for the company. Everyone who works for a company creates value. It is the responsibility of leaders to make sure that people understand their individual value contribution.

## Final Thoughts

Leaders of companies driven by people need to change their mind-set about the concept of human capital development and management. The function of human capital development may still reside within the human resources area of a company, but the perspective has to be different. Human capital development is a strategic function, not an order-taking and strategy-execution function. Laurie Bassi, president of Human Capital Dynamics, comments that we don't need to change the label—we need to change everything else. "The label is not the problem. It's the people, the mind-set, the mission they've been given. Their mission has to change. And, probably, many of the people in those functions have to change."[13]

CEOs are at the top of the human capital value chain in their respective companies. They set the stage for how the company will use and develop its people. They emphasize the importance of why people need to understand how they create value and how they contribute to the firm's results. CEOs of the future may well institute the concept of "chief people officer," whose mission would be to develop the human capital strategy for the company and ensure that the strategy is executed throughout the company. No matter what the position is called or how it is structured, the message is the same: Companies must make human capital development an essential strategic imperative.

## CHAPTER RECAP

### Workplace Trends

- CEOs are being required to manage velocity, given the unprecedented time pressure to produce specific, measurable results.

- Visionary leaders are placing importance on creating a system of measurement for intangibles that can ultimately be used as a tool to enhance the value of the firm.

- Companies that make their products and services accessible in the community are leaving a legacy of stewardship.

### Summary of Key Ideas

- CEO recruiters tap into companies that have a proven record to not only develop leaders but provide them with direct experience running business units.

- CEOs who wait too long to take action may lose business opportunities to enthusiastic and technologically savvy competitors.

- Leaders need to cultivate their best competencies so they can more effectively serve their various stakeholders.

- CEOs need to endorse the establishment of human capital management practices. If they are not driven from the top, the practices won't be taken seriously.

- Placing importance on tracking and analyzing nonfinancial measures is a corporate value.

- Leaders who contribute in the community by being board members of nonprofit associations can contribute human capital strategies.

- Firms that give back to the community are able to expand their market reach by being of service to those who otherwise lack access.

- Firms that are driven by intangible assets must have leadership that is focused on their people.

## Thinking Points

- How does your CEO and executive team manage velocity?

- What needs to be done for your firm to institutionalize human capital management practices?

- Who within your firm is in the best position to create a system for measuring human capital? Should this be comanaged by different people?

- Are your company's leaders serving on nonprofit boards in your community? How can they use their knowledge and expertise about human capital to benefit these nonprofit associations?

- How does your firm give to companies or individuals that don't have access to your products and services?

# Going to the Next Level: Human Capital as an Investment in Your Firm

When people buy stock in your company, they are investing their financial capital in your company and thereby own—that is, have equity in—a piece of the firm. They expect to realize a return on their investment at some point in the future. Assuming they are value investors, not day traders, they are committing their financial capital in your company for an indeterminate period of time. In effect, they are partnering with your company, betting on its future growth and success.

Companies that have such financial investors have responsibilities to fulfill. They are accountable to run the company to the best of their ability. Their focus is on some combination of building revenue, enhancing productivity, and increasing profitability. They are also committed to enhancing the value of their human capital when they understand the value equation between human capital and growth of the firm. (The connection between human capital practices and share price was examined in Chapter 4.) Although it is not yet a universal practice, equity analysts may eventually factor in more information on intangibles. John Hover, chairman of the board of U.S. Trust Private Equity Funds, thinks that equity analysts will increasingly evaluate human capital factors. Elements such as "retention and turnover rates, for example, will be reflected in [the analysts'] earnings estimate for the stock and therefore will affect the price."[1]

There is another side to this equation. When people commit to work for your company they, too, have made a decision to invest in your company. They are investing their human capital with the expectation of getting a return on their investment in the form of new experiences that they can add to their work portfolio. They can make new contacts and expand their network, which will enhance the value of their human capital. They can learn new technologies or methodologies that also add to their professional value.

Understanding that your people are investing in your company is yet another shift in mind-set for those who develop and manage human capital strategies. When you realize that your people are investing in you as much as you may feel you are investing in them, it becomes a much more mutually beneficial equation. The firm is responsible for giving its people the best experiences possible so that they can add to their portfolio. At the same time, your people are investing their best efforts into helping the company achieve increased revenue, productivity, or profitability. This concept works for talent. It works for free agents. But it doesn't work for labor or wage slaves.

## $W$ORKPLACE TREND

*The people who work for you are investing their human capital in your company.*

The idea of your workers investing their human capital in your company is a very different proposition from the one we have been accustomed to in bureaucratic and hierarchical companies of the past. In those firms, people are an expense, and training is an expense. People are viewed as labor, not as talent. In that scenario, it wouldn't be possible to think of workers as human capital investors in the business.

The question becomes, Do you view your people as investors? By distinguishing between labor and talent, you have most of what you need to fully embrace this proposition of your people as investors. By making the analogy between your human capital investors and your financial capital investors, you will be able to shift your mind-set the rest of the way.

## The Human Capital–Ownership Equation

In his book *Human Capital: What It Is and Why People Invest in It,* Thomas O. Davenport observes: "A worker who acts like a human capital investor will place his or her investable capital where it can earn the highest return."[2] People who consider working for your firm will evaluate how their contributions will add value to your firm and how your firm will add value to them. When both sides of the equation are balanced, it is a win-win situation for the worker and the firm. If it is unbalanced in some way, it distorts the value proposition for one side or the other.

**❝** *People who consider working for your firm will evaluate how their contributions will add value to your firm and how your firm will add value to them.* **❞**

## Stock Options

Some companies partially compensate their human capital investors by granting them options. Staying with our balanced value equation, if people are willing to risk their time and brains and experience in your firm, the company ought to be willing to risk some future equity capital in its people. When companies view their people as investors in their firms, one of the consequences is that the human resources function has to take on more of an investor relations role.[3]

This is an interesting proposition. The investor relations function has tended to be one that is committed to providing financial investors with any information they need related to their investment in the company. Human resources is more procedural and compliance oriented. It is not perceived as a resource to serve its constituency, that is, the human capital investors.

## Psychological Ownership

This human-capital-as-investor model further implies that your workers (that is, your human capital investors) own a part of your company while they're working for you. When this is the case, a much higher probability exists of commitment and buy-in, as mentioned in an earlier chapter. Workers can have a psychological sense of ownership in a company. If your corporate values and goals are aligned with their personal expectations, this feeling of ownership emerges.[4]

In fact, it is much more likely that your employees could feel more psychologically vested in your company than do financial equity investors, who are connected to your firm more through their monthly brokerage statement. The steps your company takes to create that psychological buy-in is an important ingredient in the equation, as it is much more of an emotional connection than anything else. You won't see it written in a company policy manual or a mission statement. It's a feeling that comes from belonging to something.

## The Role of Community in the Firm

People who have a sense of belonging at their place of work are more committed to high performance and the overall success of the firm. The sense of community that comes from this feeling of belonging is something that some strive to create. It is an integral part of the corporate culture. Community doesn't mean that everyone on the job has to be good friends and go to parties together every week. It means that people cultivate shared interests with their coworkers and build relationships from these points in common.

The water cooler or coffee room has served as the informal gathering point for connecting coworkers. People gravitate to these locations to take a break, to chat with friends, and to find out what's going on around the company. It is the place where they maintain an association with coworkers whom they may not see regularly during the normal course of their day.

In the digital age, the water cooler has been supplanted in part by technology. As noted in Chapter 8, people maintain one-to-one contact easily through cell phones; at the click of a speed-dial button, you can find the person you're looking for, regardless of where that person is located physically at the moment. Internet chat rooms and e-mail are other ways to maintain contact. Instant messaging is a way that people can pop in and connect with you when you're online. What's missing in these connections are visual and audio real-time observations.

Those are some of the informal ways that people build communities. In our dispersed, virtual world, it is important for managers to proactively build community in their firms. This shouldn't be left to chance. Community is an important part of corporate culture and organizational capital.

    **66** *Community is an important part of corporate culture and organizational capital.* **99**

Community building is harder to do in hierarchical organizations. People worry whether it is "politically correct" to connect with people at different levels of the organization. But developing community is one of the ways that your company can cultivate that psychological buy-in that results in a feeling of ownership. This is a powerful process that has an even more powerful outcome when done right.

Community building can backfire if your company has rigid hierarchies or is a toxic firm. The community still develops, but instead of being a positive force for psychological buy-in, it is a negative dynamic for everything from rebelliousness to dissent to disharmony. When people feel disempowered, they use their community to express their frustration and hostility, which can have a negative, viral effect on other employees, particularly if the disenfranchised ones are liked and respected.

## Impact of the Physical Environment

New economy firms populated by knowledge workers may want to consider creating new physical environments to match their changing organizational structures. The physical workspace should be flexible to account for the transiency of the workforce in a wireless world. Remote employees, strategic alliances, unconventional work hours, and other changes are becoming the norm, not the exception, and the physical "plant" can accommodate these needs.

Offices need sufficient technological sophistication so that their people can be comfortable sharing files over a network or walking in from another location and be connected via their laptop. Technological innovations need to match your company's business strategy and the image that you want to have in the market. If you work on-site with clients that are technologically savvy, your physical environment needs to be technologically supportive.

The office is no longer the place where people are required to come to work. It has evolved into a hub—a place where people can physically touch base and connect with each other. Physical office space can also reflect a company's culture and immediately draw in employees and visitors. Space that reflects the spirit of a company reinforces its values and morale.[5]

A reconfigured physical environment can also help to build community. Gensler, a global architecture, design, and strategic-consulting firm, designed a series of "hearths" for Shaklee's San Francisco headquarters. Employees informally gather and connect in the hearths as they get mail or coffee and make copies.[6]

# Building Community

What can you do to create the environment of community that will result in the strongest psychological buy-in? Much of the answer is found in your corporate culture. For purposes of this discussion, let's assume that you have a strong, human capital-centric corporate culture. You've put into place many of the principles discussed in previous chapters. You embrace the concept of free agency as the future employment model and understand that free agents are looking to build employment experiences that add to their portfolio.

## How to Treat Your People

Treat your people as you would your financial investors, which means that you understand the balanced human capital–ownership equation discussed earlier. You probably treat your financial investors as important to the future of your firm, keeping them informed of your firm's financial performance and future goals. Publicly held companies that are followed by the investment community have conference calls every quarter in which they go into detail about the company's financial results and the expectations for the following quarter. How can you adapt that concept to human capital investors?

Some companies have open-book management styles whereby they make their financials available to their people. Some firms swear by the effectiveness of this, claiming that it results in stronger employee commitment. You may not be prepared to go that far at first, but instead you can hold quarterly meetings with your people to discuss the highlights of the prior quarter's financials. You could also present your objectives for the following quarter, so that your workers understand the current corporate direction.

## Reward People Who Take Chances

Innovation happens when workers feel comfortable taking chances in their company. People who feel put down or demeaned will never feel comfortable taking risks. Managers should hold informal brainstorming sessions on a regular basis, depending on their functional area of responsibility. The purpose of these meetings is to generate ideas, whether they relate to manufacturing productivity, new product ideas, or business development.

The ground rules for these meetings are simple: (1) Everyone is included, from the department or divisional head to the support staff. (2) No idea is a bad idea. Record all ideas on a white board or flipcharts. (3) Once the ideas have been aired, facilitate a discussion relating to the ideas that best suit a particular strategy you may be working on. If these sessions are conducted on a truly open basis, you will be surprised what happens. The people you least expect will have some great implementable ideas.

Reward your people will small gifts—small cash awards or certificates for Starbucks or your local movie theatre. People will be pleased with the small gifts, but *everyone* will feel good about the team spirit that generates these ideas. At a later time, it would be appropriate to recognize your teammates in a companywide forum.

Many of these ideas about creating psychological buy-in sound like common courtesies and reflect what was discussed at the beginning of the book. When you treat people the way they want to be treated, magic can happen. Making psychological buy-in and a strong community important to your firm will go a long way to acknowledging your people—your human capital—as investors.

## Final Thoughts

The more your people understand how they contribute value, the more closely aligned they are with your firm. The value equation connects their specific job position with the company's goals. The quarterly financial meeting is an appropriate time and place to reinforce these linkages. Not only will it reinforce individual value propositions, but it will also give people the opportunity to see how their coworkers' jobs fit in. The more people who understand these connections, the more valuable the connections are to the community structure.

People want to be a part of something. Companies that encourage individual value creation are highly attractive to talent. Talent gravitates to firms where they know they are viewed as worthy and important human assets. Knowing *how* they contribute value not only validates them but envelops them into the community of the company. When this happens, human capital truly does become a firm's strongest asset.

## CHAPTER RECAP

### Workplace Trend

- The people who work for you are investing their human capital in your company.

### Summary of Key Ideas

- Companies are committed to enhancing the value of their human capital when they understand the value equation between human capital and the growth of the firm.

- People who consider working for your firm will evaluate how their contributions will add value to your firm and how your firm will add value to them.

- Community is an important part of corporate culture and organizational capital.

### Thinking Points

- Do you view your people as investors?

- Do your people have a sense of "belonging" at your company?

- What are you doing to build community in your firm?

# Valuing People Audit<sup>SM</sup>

The Valuing People Audit<sup>SM</sup> (VPA) provides a system to measure the strengths of your company's human capital strategies. The VPA appraises your firm's strengths and weaknesses and identifies areas where you can make improvements. The uniqueness of this approach is that it is strategic, not tactical.

Your first step is to complete the VPA and understand the areas in which you need to make improvement. As results will differ among companies and industries, no evaluation rankings are included. You'll know where you need to make changes just by working through the assessment.

Rank your company based on the following scale of 1 to 5:
5 = Strongly agree
4 = Often agree
3 = Sometimes agree
2 = Occasionally agree
1 = Rarely agree

1. _____ Human capital and valuing people are burning priorities for your CEO/President.

2. _____ Your HR executive is a strategic ally of your CEO.

3. _____ Your HR executive participates strategically in your firm's executive committee.

4. _____ Your CFO, head of HR, and head of strategic planning meet regularly.

5. _____ Your executive committee strategizes about human capital by looking at trends that affect your company and your industry.

6. _____ Your board understands the importance of human capital and valuing people.

7. _____ Your people clearly understand your company's mission and values.

8. _____ The importance of valuing people is communicated with alignment between words and actions.

9. _____ Your executives effectively communicate the firm's human capital vision and obtain commitment from their people.

10. _____ Your managers give their people opportunities to shine.

11. _____ Your firm has a strategy for measuring human capital recording, tracking, and analyzing measures (such as those presented in Chapters 4 and 5).

12. _____ You proactively match the right people to the right jobs.

13. _____ You assess the optimal behavior, attitudes, and interpersonal skills to effectively do specific jobs.

14. _____ Your managers motivate by matching their styles to those of their people.

15. _____ Your company provides an effective environment for creativity and innovation.

16. _____ Your people are encouraged to take risks—even with the possibility of making mistakes.

17. _____ Your company has established benchmarks to track and measure progress in human capital issues.

18. _____ You encourage new ideas to improve old methods.

19. _____ You provide appropriate technology training for your nontechnology staff.

20. _____ Your managers cut people only as a last resort.

21. \_\_\_\_ Your managers proactively work with their people on employee development plans.

22. \_\_\_\_ Your managers encourage professional and personal development, even if it means that their people may move into other positions.

23. \_\_\_\_ Your firm has a corporate strategy for training.

24. \_\_\_\_ Your firm provides coaching and other support to newly promoted managers.

25. \_\_\_\_ Your people understand exactly how they contribute value to your company.

If you have any questions about your results, feel free to send e-mail to lisa@valuing-people.com. You also can complete this assessment on the Valuing People Web site at <www.valuing-people.com>. This Web-based assessment is more detailed and contains additional questions about your company (revenue size, number of people, industry, mission, and so on). On completion of the assessment, you will receive an evaluation and basic feedback about your human capital strategy.

## Introduction

1. Bernard Wysocki, Jr., "In the U.S. Trade Arsenal, Brains Outgun Brawn," *Wall Street Journal*, 10 April 2000, p. A1.

## Chapter 1. Human Capital Is the Hub

1. Nicholas Stein, "Measuring People Power," *Fortune*, 2 October 2000, citing Hay Group Vice President Mel Stark, coleader of this survey.
2. Watson Wyatt Worldwide, "Human Capital Index: Linking Human Capital and Shareholder Value." <www.watsonwyatt.com>
3. David Clinton, "New Front in the War for Talent," *Financial Times*, 2 July 2001, p. 9.
4. Statement of David M. Walker, comptroller general of the United States, U.S. General Accounting Office, "Managing Human Capital in the 21st Century," 9 March 2000, p. 6. Document GAO/T-GGD-00-77.
5. Jeff Nash, "The New Market in Human Capital," *Money*, 1 September 2001, p. 26.
6. "Patent That Thought," *Across the Board*, April 1999, p. 5.
7. Rosabeth Moss Kanter, *Forbes ASAP*, 30 November 1998, p. 219.
8. Kevin Freiberg and Jackie Freiberg, *Nuts! Southwest Airlines' Crazy Recipe for Business and Personal Success* (Austin, TX: Bard Press, 1996), 107.

## Chapter 2. Bridging the Generations

1. Information from this section has been derived from many articles in various periodicals. Two excellent resources are J. Walker Smith and Ann Clurman, *Rocking the Ages: The Yankelovich Report on Generational Marketing* (New York: Harper Business, 1997), which has a marketing focus, and Ron Zemke, Claire Raines, and Bob Filipczak, *Generations at Work: Managing the Clash of Veterans, Boomers, Xers and Nexters in Your Workplace* (New York: Amacom, 2000), which focuses on managing across generations.
2. Benjamin Soskis, "Fall to Grace," *New Republic*, 29 January 2001, p. 12.

3. Some demographers have cut off this generation around 1997, but based on birth levels, Gen Y was still growing in 2001.

4. Arlie Russell Hochschild, "Coming of Age, Seeking an Identity," *New York Times*, 8 March 2000, p. H1.

5. Don Tapscott, "Minds over Matter," *Business 2.0,* March 2000. <www.business2.com>

6. Brian O'Reilly, "Meet the Future," *Fortune,* 24 July 2000, p. 144.

7. Mark L. Alch, "The Workers of the Net Generation," *Futurific,* January 2000, p. 10.

8. Rebecca Gardyn, "Who's the Boss?" *American Demographics,* September 2000, p. 52.

9. Hochschild, "Coming of Age."

10. Weld Royal, "Countdown to the Great Labor Shortage," *New York Times,* 22 August 2001, p. G1.

11. Tapscott, "Minds over Matter."

12. "The Next Big Singles Market," *Forecast,* 20 August 2001, p. 1.

13. Nadine Joseph, Andrea Cooper, Tara Weingarten, "Down the Aisle," *Newsweek,* 20 July 1998, p. 54.

14. Nina Munk, "Finished at Forty," *Fortune,* 1 February 1999, p. 50

15. "Brain Drain," *Business Week,* September 20, 1999, p. 112.

16. Mary Williams Walsh, "Reversing Decades-Long Trend, Americans Retiring Later in Life," *New York Times,* 16 February 2001, p. A1.

17. Fred Brock, "The Growing Roster of the Unretired," *New York Times,* 4 July 1999, p. BU7.

18. "Brain Drain."

19. Alison Maitland, "The Benefits of Going Gradually," *Financial Times,* 2 August 2000, p. 23.

20. Alison Maitland, "An Alternative to Early Retirement," *Financial Times,* 26 June 2001, p. 9.

21. Kris Maher, "How Lands' End Keeps Holiday Workers in Stock," *Wall Street Journal,* 14 December 2000, p. B1.

22. Clare Ansberry, "The Gray Team," *Wall Street Journal,* 5 February 2001, p. A1.

## Chapter 3. Who Are Your People Anyway?

1. Rebecca Gardyn, "Who's the Boss?" *American Demographics,* September 2000, p. 52.

2. "Temp Workers Have Lasting Effect," *Wall Street Journal,* 1 February 2001, p. A1.

3. Aaron Bernstein, "Now, Temp Workers Are a Full-Time Headache," *Business Week,* 31 May 1999, p. 46.

4. Dan Pink's comments are from an interview with the author. Also see Daniel H. Pink, *Free Agent Nation* (New York: Warner Books, 2001).

5. Stan Davis and Christopher Meyer, *Blur: The Speed of Change in the Connected Economy* (Reading, MA: Perseus Books, 1998), pp. 156–60.

6. Harriet B. Presser, "Toward a 24-Hour Economy," *Science,* 11 June 1999, p. 1778.

7. Kemba J. Dunham, "Telecommuters' Lament," *Wall Street Journal,* 31 October 2000, p. B1.

8. Sana Siwolop, "Offices without Walls, or Borderlines," *New York Times,* 23 August 2000, p. G1.

9. Bill Breen, "Where Are You on the Talent Map?" *Fast Company,* January 2001, p. 102.

10. Steven Greenhouse, "Foreign Workers at Their Highest Level in Seven Decades," *New York Times,* 4 September 2000, p. A1.

11. "Battle for Brains," *Financial Times,* 12–13 August 2000, p. 6.

12. David Champion, "The Curse of the Immobile Worker," *Harvard Business Review,* May/June 1999, p. 17.

13. Deborah Hargreaves, "Immigration: Rocky Road from Control to Management," *Financial Times,* 12 October 2000, p. 4.

14. Presser, "Toward a 24-Hour Economy."

15. Daniel Costello, "Incidents of 'Desk Rage' Disrupt America's Offices," *Wall Street Journal,* 15 January 2001, p. B1.

16. Thomas A. Stewart, "Whom Can You Trust? It's Not So Easy to Tell," *Fortune,* 12 June 2000. <www.fortune.com>

17. Harvey Mackay, *Swim with the Sharks without Being Eaten Alive . . .* (New York: Morrow, 1988).

18. Reed Abelson, "A Network of Their Own," *New York Times,* 27 October 1999, p. C1.

19. Catherine Banat, interview with author.

20. James P. Masciarelli, "Using Your Board's 'Relationship Capital'," *Corporate Board,* July 2000, p. 6.

## Chapter 4. Valuing Human Capital

1. Jeremy Rifkin, *The Age of Access: The New Culture of Hypercapitalism, Where All of Life Is a Paid-For Experience* (New York: J. P. Tarchner, 2001), p. 4.

2. Laurie J. Bassi, interview with author.

3. Robert K. Elliott, interview with author.

4. Robert K. Elliott, "Human Resource Measurement," unpublished paper, 24 April 2001.

5. See, for example, Alan M. Webber, "New Math for a New Economy," *Fast Company*, January/February 2000, p. 214; and Thomas A. Stewart, "Accounting Gets Radical," *Fortune*, 16 April 2001, p. 184.

6. One of the outgrowths of Lev's work with this group was a book on intangibles: Baruch Lev, *Intangibles: Management, Measurement, and Reporting* (Washington, DC: Brookings Institution Press, 2001).

7. Baruch Lev, interview with author.

8. Laurie J. Bassi, et al., "Measuring Corporate Investments in Human Capital," in Margaret M. Blair and Thomas A. Kochan, editors, *The New Relationship: Human Capital in the American Corporation*, (Washington, DC: Brookings Institution Press, 2000), p. 336.

9. Thomas A. Stewart, "Accounting Gets Radical," *Fortune*, 16 April 2001, p. 184.

10. Darrell Rigby, "Downside of Downsizing," *Financial Times*, 13 August 2001.

11. John Markoff, "Bill Gates's Brain Cells, Dressed Down for Action," *New York Times*, 25 March 2001, p. BU1.

12. Joff Wild, "A Yawning Gap That Too Many Companies Fail to Recognise," *Financial Times*, Intellectual Property/Chartered Director Supplement, 21 June 2001, p. III.

13. Bill Birchard, "Intangible Assets Plus Hard Numbers Equals Soft Finance," *Fast Company*, October 1999, p. 316.

14. Floyd Norris, "Seeking Ways to Value Intangible Assets," *New York Times*, 22 May 2001, p. C2.

15. Financial Accounting Standards Board, *Business Reporting Research Project*. <www.fasb.org>

16. Margaret M. Blair and Steven M.H. Wallman, *Unseen Wealth: Report of the Brookings Task Force on Intangibles* (Washington, DC: Brookings Institution Press, 2001), pp. 19, 55.

17. Lev, *Intangibles*, p. 127.

18. David Stamps, "Measuring Minds," *Training*, May 2000, p. 76.

19. For further details, please see <www.skandia.com>.

20. Skandia, "Human Capital in Transformation, Intellectual Capital Prototype Report," 1998. <www.skandia.com/EN/IR/annualreports.shtml>

21. Laurie J. Bassi et al., "Profiting from Learning: Do Firms' Investments in Education and Training Pay Off?" ASTD/Saba White paper, 2000.

22. Laurie J. Bassi et al., "Human Capital Investments and Firm Performance," unpublished paper, 2001.

23. Marcus Buckingham and Curt Coffman, *First, Break All the Rules: What the World's Greatest Managers Do Differently* (New York: Simon & Schuster, 1999), p. 28.

24. Bassi et al., *The New Relationship: Human Capital in the American Corporation*, pp. 338–41.

25. Ibid., pp. 342–53.

26. "The Value Creation Index," Cap Gemini Ernst & Young Center for Business Innovation, 2000. <www.cbi.cgey.com/publdocs/new_vci.pdf>

27. Walker, "Managing Human Capital."

28. U.S. General Accounting Office, "Human Capital: Key Principles from Nine Private Sector Organizations," January 2000, Document GAO/T-GGD-00-28, pp. 2–4.

29. Ibid., p. 17.

30. Jim Rohwer, "The Numbers Game: How Much Is Talent Worth to the Economy?" *Fortune*, 22 November 1999, p. 263.

31. Jacque Fitz-enz, *The ROI of Human Capital: Measuring the Economic Value of Human Performance* (New York: AMACOM, 2000), excerpted in *Tooling and Production*, August 2000, p. 28.

32. "What's a Worker Worth?" *Business Week*, 11 October 1999, p. F4.

33. Watson Wyatt Worldwide, "Human Capital Index." <www.watsonwyatt.com>

34. Dennis C. Carey and Marc A. Feigen, "Before Your M&A Deal, Do a Human Capital Audit," *Directors & Boards*, Spring 1999, p. 47.

## Chapter 5.  The Art and Science of Attracting Talent

1. Elizabeth G. Chambers et al., "The War for Talent," *McKinsey Quarterly*, no. 3, 1998, p. 44.

2. Elizabeth L. Axelrod, Helen Handfield-Jones, and Timothy A. Welsh, "War for Talent, Part Two," *McKinsey Quarterly*, no. 2, 2001.

3. Brigic McMenamin, "Lies and Whispers," *Forbes*, 4 October 1999, p. 72.

4. Stephen Overell, "The Art of the Creative Résumé," *Financial Times*, 8 August 2001, p. 8.

5. Shelly Branch, "The 100 Best Companies to Work for in America," *Fortune*, 11 January 1999, p. 118.

6. Robert Levering and Milton Moskowitz, "The 100 Best Companies to Work For," *Fortune*, 10 January 2000, p. 82.

7. Robert Levering and Milton Moskowitz, "The 100 Best Companies to Work For," *Fortune*, 8 January 2001.

8. Watson Wyatt Worldwide, "Competing in a Global Economy." <www.watsonwyatt.com>

9. Ron Winslow and Carol Gentry, "Health-Benefits Trend: Give Workers Money, Let Them Buy a Plan," *Wall Street Journal*, 8 February 2000, p. A1.

10. Jock McDonald, "The Boom in Employee Ownership," *Inc.*, August 2000, p. 106.

11. Fiona Harvey, "Of Chocolates and Profit Sharing," *Financial Times,* 26 July 2000, p. 10.

12. Sara Rimer, "Prized Ice Cream Jobs Create Extended Family," *New York Times,* 25 July 1999, p. 14.

13. Peter Marsh, "A Share in Corporate Success," *Financial Times,* 24 January 2000, p. 9.

14. Daniel Roth, "My Job at The Container Store," *Fortune,* 10 January 2000. <www.fortune.com>

15. Jonathan Karp, "Sri Lanka Keeps Victoria's Secret," *New York Times,* 13 July 1999, p. B1.

16. Cora Daniels and Carol Vinzant, "The Joy of Quitting," *Fortune,* 7 February 2000, p. 199.

17. Kemba J. Dunham, "Employers Seek Ways to Lure Back Laid-Off Workers When Times Improve," *Wall Street Journal,* 19 June 2001, p. B1.

18. Scott Kirsner, "Hire Today, Gone Tomorrow?" *Fast Company,* August 1998, p. 136.

19. Polly LaBarre, "Andy Brown Wants You!" *Fast Company,* June 1999, p. 64.

20. Levering and Moskowitz, "100 Best Companies," 2001.

21. Saltz Shamis & Goldfarb, as reported by Eric Matson, "How to Get a Piece of the Action," *Fast Company,* October 1996, p. 90.

22. Daniel H. Pink, "The Talent Market," *Fast Company,* August 1998, p. 87.

23. Michael Lewis, *Next: The Future Just Happened* (New York: W. W. Norton, 2001).

## Chapter 6. Organizational Capital

1. "Revenge of the 'Managers'," *Business Week,* 12 March 2001, p. 60.

2. "The Slow Death of Boeing Man," *Economist,* 18 March 2000, p. 29.

3. Virginia Munger Kahn, "The Electronic Rank and File," *New York Times,* 8 March 2000, p. G1.

4. Alison Maitland, "From Dead-End Job to Bright Career," *Financial Times,* 3 September 2001, p. 7.

5. Julie Flaherty, "Suggestions Rise from the Floors of U.S. Factories," *New York Times,* 18 April 2001, p. C1.

6. Michael E. Gordon and Lowell Turner, *Transnational Cooperation among Labor Unions* (Ithaca, NY: ILR Press/Cornell University Press, 2000) abstracted in *Future Survey,* April 2001, p. 19.

7. Robert Taylor, "Workers Unite on the Internet," *Financial Times,* 11 May 2001, p. 9.

8. Amanda J. Ahlstrand, Laurie J. Bassi, and Daniel P. McMurrer, "Workplace Education for Low-Wage Workers," ASTD Study, March 2001.

9. Scott Thurm, "Cisco Helps Train a Union's Workers in the Web's Ways," *Wall Street Journal,* 3 July 2001, p. B1.

10. Clare Ansberry, "By Resisting Layoffs, Small Manufacturers Help Protect Economy," *Wall Street Journal,* 6 July 2001, p. A1.

11. Daniel Goleman, *Working with Emotional Intelligence* (New York: Bantam Books, 1998), p. 6.

12. Bill J. Bonnstetter, interview with author.

13. Mortimer Adler, *How to Speak, How to Listen* (New York: Scribner, 1997).

14. Questions adapted from a Target Training International, Ltd. assessment. <www.ttidisc.com>

## Chapter 7. Employee Development

1. Robert M. Williams, interview with author.

2. These motivating attitudes adapted from a Target Training International, Ltd. assessment. <www.ttidisc.com>

3. Kim Cross, "Does Your Team Measure Up?" *Business 2.0,* 12 June 2001, p. 22.

4. Carol Hymowitz and Matt Murray, "Raises and Praise or Out the Door," *Wall Street Journal,* 21 June 1999, p. B1.

5. Anna Muoio, "Cisco's Quick Study," *Fast Company,* October 2000, p. 287.

6. Adrian Michaels, "Companies Get Bitten by the Learning Bug," *Financial Times,* Business Education Supplement, 3 April 2000, p. 1.

7. Jeanne C. Meister, "Savvy e-Learners Drive Revolution in Education," *Financial Times,* Business Education Supplement, 3 April 2000, p. 2.

8. William T. Brooks, interview with author.

9. Colleen O'Connor, "High Touch for High Tech," *Business 2.0,* February 2000, p. 219.

10. Joannie Schrof and Stacey Schultz, "Melancholy Nation," *US News & World Report,* 9 March 1999, p. 56.

11. Joann S. Lublin, "Mergers Often Trigger Anxiety, Lower Morale," *Wall Street Journal,* 16 January 2001, p. B1.

12. Carol Hymowitz and Rachel Emma Silverman, "Can Workplace Stress Get Worse? *Wall Street Journal,* 16 January 2001, p. B1.

13. Stephen Overell, "The Skill of Thriving Under Pressure," *Financial Times,* 9 January 2001, p. 13.

14. Janet Raloff, "Does Light Have a Dark Side? Nighttime Illumination Might Elevate Cancer Risk," *Science News,* 17 October 1999, p. 248.

15. Sue Shellenbarger, "Rising Before Dawn, Are You Getting Ahead or Just Getting Tired?" *Wall Street Journal,* 17 February 1999, p. B1.

16. "Why Early Means Surly," *New Scientist,* 6 November 1999, p. 7.

17. Rick Marin, "Is This the Face of a Midlife Crisis?" *New York Times*, 24 June 2001, p. ST1.

18. Christie Aschwanden, "Gene Cheats," *New Scientist*, 15 January 2000, p. 24.

19. Sharon Begley, "Are We Getting Smarter?" *Newsweek*, 23 April 2001, p. 50.

20. Brandon Mitchener, "Controlling a Computer by the Power of Thought," *Wall Street Journal*, 14 March 2001, p. B1.

## Chapter 8.  Virtual Capital: The Human-Technology Interface

1. George Gilder, "Bandwidth Abundance," *Forbes*, 6 July 1998. <www.forbes.com>

2. Zhenya Gene Senyak, "Shop Talks," *Business 2.0*, 13 June 2000, p. 187.

3. Timothy F. Bresnahan, Erik Brynjolfsson, and Lorin M. Hitt, "Technology, Organization, and the Demand for Skilled Labor," in Margaret M. Blair and Thomas A. Kochan, editors, *The New Relationship: Human Capital in the American Corporation* (Washington, DC: Brookings Institution Press, 2000), pp. 145–93.

4. William T. Brooks, interview with author.

5. Regina Fazio Maruce, "The Electronic Negotiator," *Harvard Business Review*, January-February 2000, p. 16.

6. Lisa Guernsey, "Hard Hat, Lunch Bucket, Keyboard," *New York Times*, 14 December 2000, p. G1.

7. Ann Eisenberg, "The World Through PC-Powered Glasses," *New York Times*, 14 December 2000, p. G1.

8. John Schwartz, "Wiring the City: Humans Won't Do," *New York Times*, 8 March 2001, p. G1.

9. "Japan's Mobile Marvel," *Business Week*, 17 January 2000, p. 88.

10. Neil McCartney, "Challenges Ahead as Networks Start Building the Future," *Financial Times*, 17 January 2001, p. 1 (supplement).

11. Katie Hafner, "Hi, Mom. At the Beep, Leave a Message," *New York Times*, 16 March 2000, p. G1.

12. Kathleen M. Eisenhardt, "Survival of the Swiftest," *Red Herring*, April 2000, p. 374.

13. Sue Shellenbarger, "For Harried Workers in the 21st Century (Six) Trends to Watch," *Wall Street Journal*, 29 December 1999, p. B1.

14. Jaron Lanier, "The Eternal Now," *Forbes ASAP*, 22 February 1999, p. 72.

15. Ray Kurzweil, *The Age of Spiritual Machines* (New York: Penguin Books, 1999), p. 103.

16. Ray Kurzweil, "Piece of Mind: Downloading Brains in the 21st Century," *Forbes ASAP,* 22 February 1999, p. 79.

17. James Glanz, "It's Only Checkers, but the Computer Taught Itself," *New York Times,* 25 July 2000, p. D1.

18. Otis Port, "Thinking Machines," *Business Week,* 7 August 2000, p. 78.

19. Jaron Lanier, "Virtually There," *Scientific American,* April 2001, p. 66.

## Chapter 9.  Developing Leadership Capital

1. Gary Strauss, "Companies Know Where to Go for a CEO," *USA Today,* 2 August 2001, p. 1.

2. Joann S. Lublin, "CEOs Depart Faster Than Ever as Boards, Investors Lose Patience," *Wall Street Journal,* 27 October 2000, p. B1.

3. Jennifer Couzin, "Tick, Tick, Tick," *Industry Standard,* 16 April 2001, p. 63.

4. Matt Murray, "As Huge Companies Keep Growing, CEOs Struggle to Keep Pace," *Wall Street Journal,* 8 February 2001, p. A1.

5. Christopher H. Browne, interview with author.

6. Tom Peters, "Rule #3—Leadership Is Confusing as Hell," *Fast Company,* March 2001, p.124.

7. Kevin Roberts, CEO of Saatchi & Saatchi, quoted in Alan M. Webber, "Trust in the Future," *Fast Company,* September 2000, p. 209.

8. Jeffrey Swartz, CEO Timberland Company, as quoted in George Gendron, "That Magic Moment," *INC,* June 2000, p. 11.

9. Carleton Fiorina, cited in David Kirpatrick, "Looking for Profits in Poverty," *Fortune,* 5 February 2001, p. 175.

10. Steffan Heuer, "A New Lease on Work," *Industry Standard,* 11 December 2000, p. 234.

11. "Outsiders Change America's Schools," *Futurific,* August 2000, p. 29.

12. Christopher H. Brown, interview with author.

13. Laurie J. Bassi, interview with author.

## Chapter 10.  Going to the Next Level: Human Capital as an Investment in Your Firm

1. John C. Hover, interview with author.

2. Thomas O. Davenport, *Human Capital: What It Is and Why People Invest in It* (San Francisco, Jossey-Bass, 1999), p. 8.

3. Donald L. Luskin, "Own Up to Your Options," *Business 2.0*, 27 June 2000.

4. John W. Hunt, "A Question of Ownership," *Financial Times*, 3 August 2001, p. 8.

5. Santa Raymond, "Offices That Send the Right Signals," *Financial Times*, 29 May 2001.

6. M. Arthur Gensler and Gervais Tompkin, "The Changing Workplace and the Next Economy," *Business of Design*, June-July 2001, p. 64.

# INDEX

If you are interested in profitably growing your company by developing the untapped value of your people, you may consider participating in a Valuing People CEO forum in your community. These confidential forums are designed to bring together leaders from different industries to develop their organizational strengths and enhance the value of their people.

As a busy CEO of a growing company, your time is valuable. Here are some of the benefits of attending one of these forums:

- You will learn how to determine the appropriate benchmarking tools to use for measuring your people's performance.

- You will network with other leaders who have insights from their companies and industries.

- You will learn how to use the Valuing People Audit<sup>SM</sup> as a management tool.

- You will identify more effective ways to recruit and retain talent —and thereby reduce your cost of attrition.

- You will learn ways to enhance your corporate culture so that it becomes a magnet for talent.

These forums are led by professional facilitators who are trained in the principles and techniques described in *Valuing People: How Human Capital Can Be Your Strongest Asset*. For information on this opportunity or other programs offered by Lisa Aldisert, please visit the Valuing People Web site at <www.valuing-people.com> or send an e-mail to lisa@valuing-people.com.